Samsung Galaxy S23 FE User Manual for Beginners and Seniors

A Complete and Simple User Guide with Useful Tips, Tricks and Navigational Screenshots to Help You Set up and Master Your New Phone Like a Pro.

Runo O. Kently

Table of Contents

Chapter One..19

Set up your Gadget 19

Begin using your phone 20

Power on your phone 20

Use the Setup Wizard to configure your phone 21

Bring your file from an old device..............................21

Lock or unlock your phone 22

Setting for side key 23

Press twice 23

Push and hold 24

Accounts 24

Adding a Google Account 24

Adding a Samsung account..25

Adding an Outlook account 25

Voicemail set up..26

Navigation..26

The navigation bar. 30

Navigation buttons 31

Navigation gesture..31

Design the home screeen 32

Applications' icons 33

Wallpaper..33

Themes..34

Icons 35

Widgets 35

Design Widgets 36

Home screen setting 36

Easy mode 39

Status bar 41

Notifications panel 42

Viewing notification panel 42

Quick settings... 43

Options for quick settings 44

Bixby.. 46

Bixby visby.. 46

Camera 47

Gallery 47

Internet 47

Modes and Routines 48

Internet security and parental restrictions.......................... 48

Always On Display 50

AOD theme... 51

Chapter Two.. 53

Biometric security 53

Face Identification... 53

Face recognition management 54

Scanning fingerprint.. 55

4

Fingerprint management................................56

The fingerprint verification settings 56

Settings for Biometrics................................57

Multiple Window 58

Window management 59

Edge panels...60

App panel..60

Configure edge panels. 62

Design and placement of edge panels............63

About edge panels 64

Enter text 65

Toolbar..65

Configure the Keyboard. 68

Make use of Samsung voice input 72

Chapter Three 73

Camera and Gallery 73

Camera...73

Navigate the camera's screen.....................74

Choose a shooting mode. 75

AR Zone..78

Space Zoom..79

Record videos 80

360 Audio recording 80

Camera settings 81

Gallery 86

Viewing photo in gallery 86

Edit photos 88

Watch video 89

Brighten Video 90

Video editing 90

Share photo and videos 92

Delete the images and videos. 92

Assemble similar photo...................................... 93

Taking screenshot 93

Swipe palm to take a screenshot 93

Screenshot settings.. 94

Screen recorder.. 95

Screen recorder's settings................................. 96

Using application... 97

Disable or remove apps 97

Search for apps 97

Sort apps 98

Create and use folders 98

Copy a folder to a Home screen........................ 99

Delete a folder 100

Game Booster 100

App settings 101

Calendars 102

Add calendars 102

Calendar alert style...103

Create an event...104

Delete an event...104

Clock 105

Alarm...106

Remove an alarm...106

creating alerts...107

Alarm setting...107

Chapter Four 108

Contacts 108

Set up a contact 109

Modify the phone number 109

Favorites 109

Transmit a contact 110

Show contacts while sharing contacts...........................111

Groups...111

Create a group. 111

Remove or include group contacts...............................112

Group message sent 112

To a group, send an email............................. 113

Eliminate a group 113

Command contacts 114

Connect contacts 114

contact import 115

Contacts for export 116

Contact sync.. 116

Delete contact... 116

Remove contact 117

Emergency contact 117

Phone.. 119

Calls 120

Create a call.. 120

Call someone from Recent Calls 120

Call someone by using Contacts. 120

Receive a call... 121

Reject the call.. 122

Reject with a message.................................. 122

Refuse a call 123

When on a call, do this................................. 123

Set the speaker or the headset to on. 123

Multitask 124

Call background 124

Pop-up menu for incoming calls 125

Manage calls 126

Call log 126

Save a contact from recent call list 126

Erase call history 127

Block a number 127

Speed dial 128

Make a call with speed dial 128

Remove a speed dial number 129

Emergency calls 129

Phone settings 130

Optional calling services 130

Place a multi-party call 130

Video calls 131

Effects for video call 131

Wi-Fi calling 132

Real Time Text (RTT) 132

Messages 134

Search for message 135

Delete conversation 135

Emergency message 136

Sharing in emergency 137

9

Message settings... 137

Notification of emergency 138

Internet.. 139

Browser tabs 140

Add a bookmark... 140

Launch a bookmark.. 140

Save a website... 140

See history.. 141

Sharing pages 141

Secret mode 142

Secret mode settings 143

Deactivate Secret mode................................. 143

Internet settings.. 143

My Files... 144

Group files.. 144

My Files Settings 145

Samsung Health 147

Before you start working out 147

Samsung Notes.. 149

Make a note 150

Voice recording 150

Edit notes 150

Option for notes 151

Note menu 152

Access settings 153

Find a settings 153

Chapter Five 154

Connections 154

Wi-Fi 154

Connect to a hidden Wi-Fi network 154

Direct Wi-Fi Direct 156

Disconnect from Wi-Fi Direct 156

Intelligent Wi-Fi settings 156

Advanced Wi-Fi settings 159

Bluetooth 160

Rename a paired device 161

Unpair from a Bluetooth device 161

Advanced Bluetooth settings 162

Dual audio 163

NFC and payment 164

Pay and Tap 164

Ultra-wideband 165

Airplane mode 165

SIM management 166

Mobile networks 168

Use of date 169

Switch on data saving 170

Check mobile data.. 170

Monitor Wi-Fi data.. 171

Mobile hotspot.. 172

Configure mobile hotspot settings.............................. 172

Auto hotspot 173

Tethering.. 174

Scanning for nearby devices 175

Ethernet 175

Network lock status 176

Connected gadgets 176

Sound and Vibration 178

sound mode 178

Mute with hand gestures... 179

Vibrations 180

Volume 181

Regulate media with volume key................................ 182

Media volume limit 182

Ringtone 183

Notification sound... 183

Notifications.. 184

Apps notifications 184

Lock screen notifications 185

Notification pop-up style 186

Do not disturb 187

Advanced setting for notification 189

Alert when phone picked up 190

Display 191

Dark mode 191

Display brightness 192

Motion smoothness 192

Eye comfort shield 193

Accidental touch protection 194

Touch sensitivity 194

Show charging information 195

Screen saver 195

Raise to wake 196

Double tap to switch on screen 196

Double-tap to switch off screen 197

Keep the device screen on while viewing 197

Using only one hand 197

Lock screen and security 198

Screen lock types 198

Set a secure screen lock 199

Find My Mobile 201

Turn on Find My Mobile... 201

Google Play Protect.. 203

Security update 203

Samsung pass... 204

Installing unidentified apps............................... 204

Password for factory data reset............................ 205

Activate SIM card lock... 205

Viewing password 206

Device administration 206

Credentials storage 207

Advanced security settings 208

Location.. 209

App permissions.. 209

Location services.. 210

Improve accuracy... 210

Recent access 211

Emergency location service 211

Accounts... 212

Add an new account 212

Account settings... 213

Delete an account 213

Backup and restoration.................................. 214

Samsung account 214

Google account 214

External storage transfer 215

Settings for Google 215

Date and time 215

Reset 216

Reset all settings 217

Reset network settings 217

Reset accessibility settings...218

Reset factory data..218

Introduction

Are you a beginner or an elderly person looking for a basic guide on setting up and using your Samsung phone?

Do you plan on keeping in touch with loved ones using any of the many APPS available on your new Samsung phone?

This book will show you how to use your Samsung phone with ease and walk you through the entire process step by step.

If you're looking to get the most out of your Samsung phone, whether you're a first-time user or an experienced veteran, this guide is for you.

This book is the complete reference for every Samsung phone user, whether you're an old pro or just getting started. You'll be taken on a journey of discovery as you learn about the smartphone's hidden potential and futuristic features.

Copyright 2023 © Runo O. Kently

Copyright 2023 © Runo O. Kently

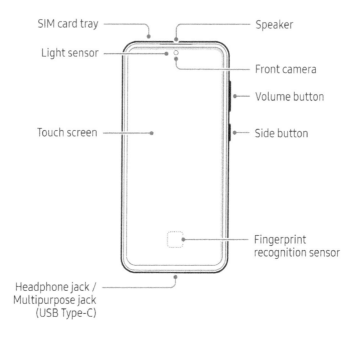

SIM card tray ——————————————— Speaker

Light sensor ————————— Front camera

Volume button

Touch screen —————— Side button

Fingerprint
recognition sensor

Headphone jack /
Multipurpose jack
(USB Type-C)

18

Chapter One

Set up your Gadget

Your device operates with nano-SIM cards. You might be able to use a SIM card that came preinstalled or an outdated SIM card. Network indicators for 5G service are based on the standards and network accessibility of your service provider. Speak to your service provider for further details.

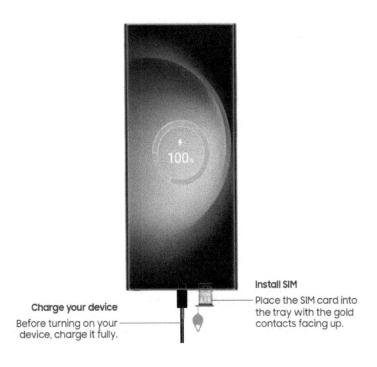

Install SIM
Place the SIM card into the tray with the gold contacts facing up.

Charge your device
Before turning on your device, charge it fully.

Begin using your phone

Power on your phone

By pressing the Side key, you can turn your smartphone on. Use caution if the device's body has been shattered or fractured. After it has been fixed, only use the appliance.

o   Pressing and holding the Side key will activate the device.

•   To turn the device off, press and hold the Side and Volume Down keys while touching ⏻ Power off. Confirm when asked.

•   To restart your smartphone, press and hold the Side and Volume Down keys at the same time. Confirm when asked.

TIP: From the Settings menu, choose ◌ Advanced features > Side key > How to power down your phone to learn more about doing so.

NOTE: A strong 5G connection and clear antennae are required for the optimal 5G performance (on the back of your smartphone). To determine whether the network is accessible, speak with your service provider.

Use the Setup Wizard to configure your phone

The first time you power on your device, the Setup Wizard will guide you through the basics of customizing it.

Simply follow the on-screen prompts to choose the language that will be your device's default, connect to a Wi-Fi network, establish accounts, choose location services, and more.

Bring your file from an old device

Download Smart Switch to move data from your old device, including contacts, pictures, music, videos, messages, notes, and calendars. Smart Switch may move your data via a PC, Wi-Fi, or a USB cord.

Visit   Samsung.com/SmartSwitch   for   more information.

1. In the Settings menu, select Bring data from old smartphone > Accounts and backup.

2. Follow the directions and pick the content you want to transfer.

Lock or unlock your phone

Use the screen lock options to protect your device. By default, the gadget locks itself when the screen shuts off. To learn more about screen locks, visit Lock screen and security.

Side key
Press to lock.
Press to turn on the
screen, and then
swipe the screen to
unlock it.

Setting for side key

Shortcuts that are assigned to the Side key can be altered.

Press twice

If you press the Side key twice, choose which function will be activated.

1. Under the Settings section, select Advanced features > Side key.

2. To use this functionality, tap twice and choose from the list below:

- Open camera quickly (the default setting)

Push and hold

When the Side key is pressed and held down, choose the function to activate.

1. Under the Settings section, select Advanced features > Side key.

2. From the Press and hold heading, choose one of the options listed below:
   - By default wake Bixby up

Accounts

Your accounts can be created and managed in accounts.

NOTE: Services like contacts, calendars, and email may be supported by accounts.

Adding a Google Account

Sign in to your Google Account to take advantage of all of your device's Android features, access your

Google Cloud Storage, use apps that you installed from your account, and more.

When you enter into a Google Account and set up a Lock screen, Google Device Protection is activated. This service needs information from your Google Account to restore your device to its factory settings. For more information, go to Google Play Protect.

1. Choose Manage accounts under Accounts and backup from the Settings menu.

2. From the Add account menu, choose Google.

Adding a Samsung account

Sign in to your Samsung account to access exclusive Samsung content and use all of Samsung's apps.

o   Choose Samsung account from the Settings menu.

Adding an Outlook account

Register for an Outlook account to access and manage your email.

1. Choose Manage accounts under Accounts and backup from the Settings menu.

2. Under Add account, choose Outlook.

Voicemail set up

You can customise your voicemail service once you've accessed it for the first time. The Phone app provides access to voicemail. Options may vary per service provider.

1. Press and hold the 1key or tap viocemail to access the voicemail from the phone app.

2. Follow the prompts to create a password, a greeting, and input your name.

Navigation

The ideal way to interact with touch displays is with light touches using either the touch pad on your finger or a capacitive stylus. If you apply excessive force to the touch screen surface or scratch it with something metallic, it could get damaged; this damage is not covered by the guarantee.

Tap

Touch something lightly to choose or launch it.

- Tap a product to select it.
- Double-tap a picture to enlarge or reduce the zoom.

Swipe

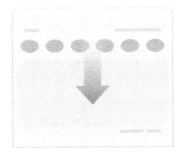

Your finger should be lightly dragged across the screen.

- Swipe the display to unlock the gadget.
- Swipe the screen to move between the Home screens or menu options.

Drag and drop

Touch and hold an object, then move it to a different location.

- To add a shortcut to an app, drag it to the Home screen.
- To reposition a widget, simply drag it there.

Scale in and out

Move your thumb and fingers closer to or farther away from each other on the screen to zoom in and out.

- By separating your thumb and forefinger on the screen, you may zoom in.
- Use your thumb and forefinger to simultaneously tap the screen to zoom out.

Tap and hold

Touch and hold things to make them active.

- Touching and holding a field will cause a pop-up menu of options to appear.

- To make changes to a Home screen, touch and hold it.

The navigation bar.

To navigate, use the navigation buttons on your smartphone or full-screen gestures.

Navigation buttons

Use the buttons on the screen's bottom for quick navigation.

1. Open the Settings program and click Display > Navigation bar > Buttons.

2. By clicking a button under Button order, you may choose which side of the screen will display the Back and Recent apps icons.

Navigation gesture

Hiding the bottom-of-the-screen navigation buttons will allow you to enjoy a screen without any interruptions. To navigate instead, swipe your device.

1. Swipe gestures can be enabled by choosing Settings > Display > Navigation bar.

2. Choose an option to customize:

• More options: Choose the sensitivity and kindness of the gesture.

• Gesture hits: Display lines at the bottom of the screen indicating the locations of each gesture to provide gesture tips.

- Move applications when hint hidden: When enabled, you can still utilize the gesture to switch between apps even when the gesture hint is disabled.

• Display keyboard hiding icon: When the device is in portrait mode, an icon in the bottom right corner of the screen will be visible. This icon will allow you to conceal the keyboard.

• Prevent the S Pen from making navigational gestures by blocking the S Pen from doing so (Galaxy S23 Ultra only).

Design the home screeen

Your device's navigation should start on the Home screen. You can put your preferred apps and widgets here in addition to making numerous Home screens, deleting screens, rearranging screens, and choosing a default Home screen.

Applications' icons

Use the icon for the app to launch it from any Home screen.

- o Under the Applications section, tap and hold an app icon, then choose ⊞ Add to Home.

- o On the Home screen, press down the finger on an app icon and choose 🗑 Remove to delete it.

NOTE: Deleting an app's icon from the Home screen simply gets rid of the icon; it doesn't get rid of the program.

Wallpaper

By choosing a favorite photo, preloaded wallpaper, or video, you may alter how the Home and Lock displays look.

1. After tapping and holding the screen on a Home screen, select 🖼 Wallpaper and style.

2. To display the wallpaper options, select one of the menus indicated below:

- Tap the images on the Home screen and Lock screen to alter them.

- Change wallpapers: Choose from the many options or download more from Samsung Themes.

- Color palette: Choose a color palette that complements the hues of your wallpaper.

- To make your wallpaper darker when it is on, enable applying Dark mode to it.

Themes

Choose a theme for your app icons, background images, and Home and Lock screens.

1. Beginning with the Home screen, tap and hold the screen.

2. Tap 🏳 Themes to browse and download available themes.

3. Choose 🔳 Menu > My stuff > Themes to examine the themes you've downloaded.

4. Choose a theme, then click Apply to make it active.

Icons

Apply numerous icon sets to replace the default icons

1. Beginning with the Home screen, tap and hold the screen.

2. By choosing 🎨 Themes > Icons, pick an icon set to preview and download.

3. Choose ☰ Menu > My items > Icons to view the icons you've downloaded.

4. After selecting an icon, press Apply to use the selected icon set.

Widgets

Add widgets to your home screens for quick access to apps or information.

1. Beginning with the Home screen, tap and hold the screen.

2. After choosing a widget set by tapping it, tap ⊞ Widgets to access it.

3. Swipe to the widget that you want to add to your home screen, then click Add.

Design Widgets

After you've created a widget, you can change where it is and how it works.

- On a Home screen, tap an option after touching and holding a widget:

  - ⊞ Create a stack by adding more widgets of the same size to the same spot on the screen.

  - 🗑 Erase: An eraser removes a widget from your screen.

  - Touch ⚙ icon modify the widget's appearance or behavior in the settings.

  - Touch ⓘ icon to examine the widget's usage, permissions, and other app details.

Home screen setting

Make your home and app screens distinctive.

1. Beginning with the Home screen, tap and hold the screen.

2. To modify, click ⚙ Settings:

- Layout of the home screen: Set up your device to have separate home and applications screens, or just a single home screen that contains all of your installed apps.

- Grid: Choose a grid to customize how icons are displayed on the Home screen.

- Grid for the apps screen: Choose a layout to determine where the icons will be positioned.

- Folder grid: Choose a layout to determine the arrangement of folders.

- On the home screen, add a media page: When enabled, slide right from the Home screen to bring up a media page. Tap to get a list of the media services that are offered.

- Display a app screen button on the Home screen so users may quickly access the Applications screen.

- Lock the Home screen's layout: Prevent items from being added to or taken away from the Home screen.

- Add newly downloaded apps to the Home screen: The Home screen will automatically add new apps.

- Hide app from Home and Apps screens: Choose the applications you want to remove from the Home and App screens. Re-enter this screen to bring back the hidden apps. Even though an app is hidden, it is still installed and is still searchable in the Finder.

- App icon badges: Enable the display of badges for programs with active alarms. There is also the option of a badge.

- Swipe down from the notification panel: Enable this option to access the notification panel by sliding down from any point.

- Change your device to landscape mode: Rotate the Home screen automatically whenever your device's orientation is changed from portrait to landscape.

- Contact Samsung support by using Samsung Members to get in touch with us.

Easy mode

The Easy mode style provides a clearer visual experience thanks to larger text and icon sizes. Switch between the default screen layout and a simpler one.

1. In the settings menu, select Display > Easy Mode.

2. To activate this feature from the Settings menu, tap . There are the following options:

- **Touch and hold delay:** Decide how long must pass before a continuous contact qualifies as a touch and hold.

- **High contrast keyboard:** Choose a keyboard with colors that are visibly distinct.

Status bar

Device information can be found on the right side of the Status bar, and notification alerts can be found on the left.

Status icons

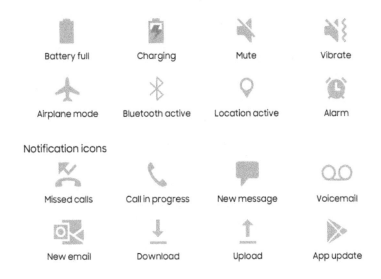

Battery full   Charging   Mute   Vibrate

Airplane mode   Bluetooth active   Location active   Alarm

Notification icons

Missed calls   Call in progress   New message   Voicemail

New email   Download   Upload   App update

TIP: From the Quick settings menu, select⋮ Additional options > Status bar to adjust the settings for the Status bar notifications.

Notifications panel

You can easily access notifications, settings, and more by launching the Notification panel.

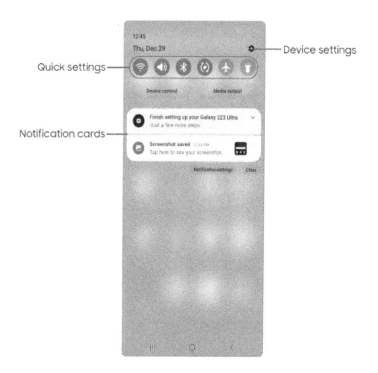

Viewing notification panel

You can reach the Notification panel from any screen.

1. Swipe down on the screen to reveal the Notification panel.

- To open something, tap it.

- To remove a single notification, slide the notice to the left or right.

- To get rid of every notice, tap Clear.

- To modify your notification settings, tap Notification settings.

2. To close the Notification panel, pull it up from the bottom of the screen or click the Back button.

Quick settings

The Notification panel provides rapid access to device functionality by using Quick settings. The icons below serve as representations of the most used Quick settings. An icon's color changes depending on whether it is active or inactive. More settings are possible for your device.

1. Dragging the Status bar lower will make the Notification panel visible.

2. Swipe down again from the top of the screen to show Quick settings.

- By tapping an icon, you can turn a quick setting on or off.

- Touch and hold the symbol to bring up the fast settings menu.

| Wi-Fi | Sound | Bluetooth | Auto rotate |

| Airplane mode | Location | Power saving | Dark mode |

Options for quick settings

The following choices can be found in the Quick settings menu.

- Search the device with the finder.

- Options for powering off and restarting are provided.

- Settings: It's simple to access the device's settings menu.

44

- ⋮More options: Alter the Quick settings or change the button layout.

- Device control is possible with approved apps like Google Home or SmartThings when they are installed.

- Manage the playback of associated audio and video devices by opening the Media panel.

- To alter the brightness of the screen, drag the brightness slider.

Bixby

Bixby is a virtual personal assistant that develops, evolves, and imitates you more and more. It gets to know your routines, helps you set up reminders based on time and location, and is included into your favorite apps. Visit Samsung.com/us/support/owners/app/Bixby to learn more.

- o While on a Home screen, press and hold the Side key.

Tips: A different route to Bixby is via the Applications list.

Bixby visby

Bixby is connected to your camera, gallery, and internet apps to make it easier for you to understand what you see. It provides contextual icons for buying, identifying landmarks, detecting QR codes, and translating.

Camera

Bixby Vision is available on the camera viewfinder to help you understand what you see.

- o Follow the instructions after selecting More > Bixby Vision from the Camera.

Gallery

Bixby Vision is compatible with images and photos saved in the Gallery app.

1. Tap a photo to open it in the gallery.

2. Touch Bixby Vision, then adhere to the guidelines.

Internet

Bixby Vision may be used to find out more information about an image you discover in the Internet app.

1. On the internet app, Tap and hold an online image to reveal a pop-up menu.

2. Choose Search with Bixby Vision and follow the prompts.

Modes and Routines

To have your device's settings change automatically based on your activities or environment, create modes and routines.

- o Hit ⊘ Modes and Routines in the Settings section to access the following pages:

- • Modes: Choose a mode based on what you're doing or where you are.

- • Routines: Set call patterns based on places or times using routines.

Internet security and parental restrictions

You may monitor and manage your digital habits by keeping track of how frequently you use programs, how many alerts you receive, and how frequently you check your smartphone on a daily basis. You can even set your gadget to help you unwind before bed.

- o From the Settings menu, choose Digital Wellbeing and parental controls for the following features:
- Touch the Dashboard to get to the following:
  - Screen time: Check the duration of time spent opening and using an app each day.
  -Notification: See the daily total of alerts a given app has sent out.
  - Times opened/Unlocked: Check out each app's daily usage statistics.
- Screen time goal: Set a limit on your screen time and assess the daily average after making your decision.
- App timer: Use app timers to set daily usage restrictions for each app.
- Driving monitor: See which applications you use the most frequently while driving while keeping an eye on your screen time using the Bluetooth in your vehicle.

- Volume monitor: Decide on a sound source so you can monitor the volume and safeguard your hearing.

- Parental controls: Keep an eye on your children's internet activity by using the Google Family Link app. You may choose apps, make content filters, keep an eye on how much time you spend on screens, and set screen time limits.

Always On Display

You may access the time and date, missed call and message alerts, and other customizable information using Always On Display without having to unlock your device (AOD).

1. From the Settings menu, select 🔒 Lock screen > Always On Display.

2. Touch 🌙 to turn on the feature, then select one of the options below:

- You can choose whether to have a clock and notifications show up when your device isn't in use.

- Clock pattern: The look and color of the clock can be changed for both the Always on Display and the Lock screen.

- Show music info: Information about the music is displayed when the FaceWidgets music controller is turned on.

- Screen orientation: Choose between portrait and landscape orientation for the AOD.

- Auto brightness: The brightness of the Always On Display can be altered automatically.

- About Always on Display: Use Always On Display to view information about the current software version and license.

AOD theme

You should use your own Always On Display themes.

1. On the Home screen, tap and hold the screen to select 🖌 Themes > AODs.

- Tap it to preview and download the AOD to your list of always-on displays.

2. Go on ▦ Menu > My items > AODs to display downloaded themes.

3. After tapping an AOD, tap Apply.

Chapter Two

Biometric security

Use biometrics to log into accounts and securely unlock your smartphone.

Face Identification

You may unlock your screen by turning on face recognition. If you want to unlock your device using your face, you must first set a pattern, PIN, or password.

- Face recognition is less secure when compared to a pattern, PIN, or password. Your device might be unlocked by someone or something that looks like you.
- Face recognition may be hampered by some conditions, like the wearing of glasses, hats, beards, or heavy makeup.
- Ensure sure your face is being registered in a well-lit area and that the camera lens is clean.

1. Facial recognition may be found under Settings > ⬤ Security and privacy > Biometrics.

2. Follow the steps to properly register your face.

Face recognition management

Enhance the personalization of facial recognition.

○ On ⬤ Security and privacy > Biometrics tab under Settings can be used to obtain face recognition.

• Erase existing faces to eliminate facial data.

• Add alternative appearance to boost recognition: Add a distinct appearance to boost facial recognition.

• Using facial recognition, you can enable or disable security.

• Remain on the Lock screen until swipe: Keep your device on the Lock screen until you swipe the screen while using facial recognition to unlock it.

- Require open eye: The only way facial recognition technology can recognize your face is if your eyes are open.

- Brighten the screen: Do this temporarily to make it easier to see your face in low light.

- Face recognition info: Learn more about using facial recognition to safeguard your device.

Scanning fingerprint

You can avoid entering a password by using fingerprint recognition in some applications.

You can use your fingerprint as an additional form of identification verification when logging into your Samsung account. To use your fingerprint to unlock your smartphone, you must first input a pattern, PIN, or password.

1. Choose Fingerprints under ⭕ Security and privacy > Biometrics > Settings.

2. Adhere to the instructions in order to register your fingerprint.

Fingerprint management

Change, add, and rename the fingerprints.

- ○ Choose ⬤ Security and privacy > Biometrics > Fingerprints under Settings to see the following settings.

- • A list of registered fingerprints is the first item on this list. Press a fingerprint to remove or rename it.

- • Added more fingerprint: Just follow the instructions to register a different fingerprint.

- • View added fingerprints: By scanning it, you can determine if your fingerprint has been saved.

The fingerprint verification settings

Use fingerprint recognition to verify your identity in compatible apps and actions.

- ○ Choose Fingerprints under ⬤ Security and privacy > Biometrics > Settings in the Settings menu.

- Using your fingerprint as authentication, you can unlock your device.

- Fingerprints are perpetually active. You may scan your fingerprint even with the screen off.

- Icon while screen is off: When the screen is off, the fingerprint icon is displayed.

- When unlocked, show a transition animation: Display an animation when using fingerprint authentication.

- Learn more about using fingerprints to safeguard your device in the fingerprint section.

Settings for Biometrics

Choose from the various biometric security options.

o Choose Settings > Security and privacy > Biometrics for the following:

- Show the unlock transition result: Use a transitional effect while unlocking your device with biometrics.

- Find out more about using biometrics to secure your device when it comes to biometric unlocking.

Multiple Window

The Window controls can be used to change the split screen display of program windows.

Split screen control

1. While on any screen, click ⊥⊥⊥ **Recent apps**

2. Click the app icon and then touch **Open in split screen view.**

3. Select application in another window to add it to the split screen view.

• Drag the mid point of the window border to adjust the window size

Window management

Window management controls how app window are shown in split screen view.

1. Drag the mid point of the window border to adjust the window size

2. Select the mid point of the window border for the option below:

• ↑↓ Switch window: Touch icon to swap between two windows

• ☆ Add app pair to: Create an application shortcut and add it to the Apps panel on the Edge screen.

Edge panels

Access the numerous customisable panels that make up the Edge panels by using the screen's edge. Applications, tasks, and contacts can all be shown in edge panels along with news, sports, and other information.

- o In Settings, choose Display > Edge panels to activate this function.

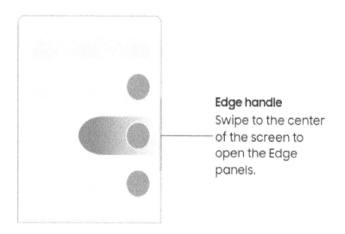

Edge handle
Swipe to the center of the screen to open the Edge panels.

App panel

The add-app button is found in the Applications section.

1. From any screen, dragging the Edge handle to the screen's center. In order to see the Applications section, swipe up.

2. To open an app's shortcuts, tap the app or pair of apps. Instead, you can tap ⋮⋮ All apps to see the whole list of apps.

- Drag the app icon from the Applications panel to the active window to bring up additional windows.

How to modify the Applications panels:

1. To change the Apps panel's appearance, drag the Edge handle to the screen's center from any screen. In order to see the Applications section, swipe up.

2. To add other apps to the Apps menu, select 🖉 Edit.

- Find the application you wish to add to the Apps panel on the left side of the screen, and then press it to drag it to an open position in the right column.

- Create a shortcut to a folder by dragging an app from the left side of the screen onto an app in the right column.

- The order of the apps can be changed by dragging each one to the desired location on the panel.

- To uninstall an app, tap ▬ Uninstall.

3. Choose ⟨ "Back" to apply changes.

Configure edge panels.

You can change each Edge panel individually.

1. One should choose ⚙ Display > Edge panels > Panels under Settings.

2. The options are as follows:

- ✅ Checkbox: Activate or deactivate each panel.

- **Edit:** Configure individual panels (if available).

- 🔍 Search for panels that are already installed or are easily installable.

- ⋮ More options:

  - Rearrange the panels by dragging them to the left or right to change their order.

  - Uninstall: Delete a downloaded Edge panel from your device.

  - Choose which panels to hide on the Lock screen when a secure screen lock is enabled.

- Visit the Galaxy Store to browse and download more Edge panels.

3. Choose ‹ "Back" to apply changes.

Design and placement of edge panels

You can change where the Edge handle is located.

- o The options listed below are accessible by selecting Handle from Settings > ⚙ Display > Edge panels:

- Edge handle: Drag to change the edge handle's position on the screen.

- Position: Choose either Right or Left to choose which side of the screen the Edge display will be on.

- By using the lock handle position feature, you may prevent the handle's position from moving when it is touched and held.

- Deciding on a color for the Edge handle's design

- Transparency: To alter the transparency of the Edge handle, use the slider.

- Size: Use the slider to alter the Edge handle's size.

- The width of the Edge handle can be modified using the slider.

- Touching the Edge handle causes it to vibrate.

About edge panels

The software version and license information for the Edge panels functionality can be viewed.

- Click Display > Edge panels > About Edge panels in the Settings menu.

Enter text

Text can be spoken aloud or entered using a keyboard.

Expand toolbar

Toolbar

The toolbar enables quick access to the keyboard's features. Options may vary per service provider.

o On the Samsung keyboard, tap ••• Expand toolbar to open the following options:

- ☺ Expression: Learn how to create unique emoji combos, GIFs, and other emoji variations.

- Take advantage of the 🗔 clipboard.

- Use a ⊟ one-handed keyboard by switching to that layout.

- Use the Samsung device's 🎤 voice input.

- Enter the ⚙ settings for the keyboard.

- Type in the text using your 𝑇𝑜 handwriting (Galaxy S23 Ultra only).

- ⌨ Split keyboard: Use a divided keyboard that is split.

- ⌨ Floating keyboard: Create a floating keyboard that can be positioned anywhere on the screen.

- Use the 🔍 search option to look for words or phrases that were used in your conversations.

- Translate: Type words or sentences into a different language using the keyboard.

- Extract text: Look for and pull the text from the stuff you've selected.

- With Samsung Pass, you can swiftly and securely access your personal information and online accounts by using biometrics.

- Grammarly: Grammarly will suggest words as you type.

- Emojis: Insert an emoji here.

- GIFs: Consist of animated GIFs.

- Use your personalized emoji as stickers with Bitmoji.

- Upload your own stickers or pick from the ones that are automatically added with Mojitok.

- You can create your own unique emoji and use it in stickers with augmented reality emoji.

- Spotify: Play music from SpotifyTM.

- Videos from YouTube should be included.

- You can alter the keyboard's height and width.

- Text editing involves cutting, copying, and pasting particular text. Find it with the use of an editing panel.

Configure the Keyboard.

Change the Samsung keyboard's preferences. Options vary depending on the service provider.

- o To access the following options, tap Settings on the Samsung keyboard:

- Languages and their variations: Choose the keyboard's style and the languages that are supported.

– To switch languages, use the Space bar to swipe left or right.

Smart typing

- Predictive text: While you type, you'll see suggested words and phrases.
- Adding emojis is advised when using predictive text.
- While you type, you can see suggested stickers: While you type, you can see suggested stickers.
- To automatically replace what you type, use the predictive text suggestions.
- Provide ideas for text repairs by highlighting faulty word spellings in red and doing so.
- Text shortcuts: Create shorthand versions of expressions you frequently use.
- Add additional customised possibilities by adding more typing options.

Layout and style

- You can display or conceal the keyboard toolbar.

- High contrast keyboard: Change the size and color of the Samsung keyboard to improve the contrast between the keys and the background.

- Theme: Decide on a layout for your keyboard's theme.

- Mode: Choose between portrait and landscape orientations.

- Size and transparency can be altered for the keyboard.

- Layout: Display numerals and special characters on the keyboard.

- If you want to change the size of the text, use the slider.

- Create your own symbols by changing the keyboard's shortcuts for them.

Additional settings

- Voice input: Configure your voice input settings and services.

- Customize feedback and motions with swipe, touch, and feedback.

- Personalized handwriting options (Galaxy S23 Ultra only).

- Text fields like search boxes and address bars can be written in using the S Pen. You can edit the text created from your handwriting with the S Pen (Galaxy S23 Ultra only).

- Enable the keyboard setting that allows screenshots to be saved to the clipboard.

- Selecting pertinent content from outside parties Make use of the extra keyboard functions.

- Reset all options to their default values: Reset the keyboard to its default configuration and remove all customizations.

- Information about the Samsung keyboard See the version and legal information for the Samsung keyboard.

- Please contact us: You can contact Samsung support through Samsung Members.

Make use of Samsung voice input

Instead of typing, enter text using your voice.

o On the Samsung keyboard, choose Voice input to have your text read aloud.

Return to keyboard

Chapter Three

Camera and Gallery

The Gallery is where you may view and edit the photographs and movies that are kept there, while the Camera app allows you to capture the highest-quality images and videos.

 Camera

Use a complete choice of expert lenses and cutting-edge video settings.

o   Click Camera under Applications.

Tips: Hit the side button twice fast to open the camera app.

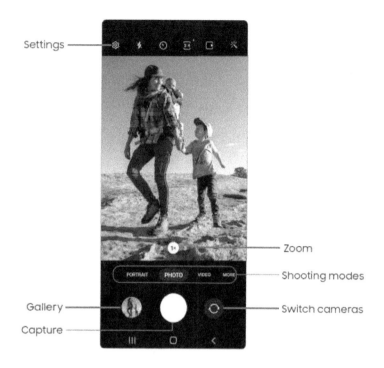

Settings

Zoom

Shooting modes

Gallery

Switch cameras

Capture

Navigate the camera's screen

Snap gorgeous photo by using the device rear and front cameras.

1. From the camera, arrange your shot using one of the possibilities provided below:

- To set the camera's focus, tap the screen where you want it to be.

- When you tap the screen, a scale of brightness appears. Slider movement will alter the brightness.

- To quickly switch between the front and back cameras, swipe up or down on the screen.

- To accurately zoom in, tap 1x and then a choice at the bottom of the screen. (Only used if using the rear camera.)

- To choose between shooting modes, move your finger up or down on the screen.

- Tap ⚙ Settings to change the camera's settings.

2. Tap ◯ Capture

Choose a shooting mode.

Choose from a range of shooting modes or let the camera choose which mode is ideal for your pictures.

o Swipe the camera's screen right and left to change between shooting modes.

- Portrait: Change the background of your photos when you take portrait shots.

75

- Let the camera determine the optimal settings for taking pictures.

- Video: Let the camera to choose the settings that work best.

- Also, choose from the different shooting modes. Tap ⊕ Add to add or delete shooting modes from the tray located at the base of the Camera interface.

- Save the Expert RAW shooting mode on your computer.

- Expert tip: While taking pictures, manually adjust the ISO sensitivity, exposure setting, white balance, and color tone.

-When taking professional-quality video recordings, manually adjust the ISO sensitivity, exposure value, white balance, and color tone.

- Single-take photography and filming: Shoot several stills and moving pictures from diverse angles.

- Panoramic: Take horizontal or vertical pictures to produce a linear image.

- At night: You can avoid using the flash by using this to take images in low light. - Food: Shoot pictures that show off the food's vivid colors.

- Ultra slow motion: Produce slow motion videos with a very high frame rate for high resolution. You can play a certain part of a video in slow motion after you've recorded it.

- Video footage should be captured at a high frame rate for slow-motion viewing.

- Hyperlapse: Create a time-lapse video from many frames-per-second snapshots. The frame rate might change depending on the scene being photographed and how the camera is moving.

- Make changes to your photographs' backgrounds when creating a portrait video.

- Director's view: Have access to a variety of high-end features, like locking onto a visible subject and switching between numerous back camera lenses.

AR Zone

All of your augmented reality (AR) features may be accessed from one place.

- ○ Choose More from the Camera menu, then tap AR Zone. The following characteristics can be found:

- • Using AR tools, create and customize your My Emoji avatar with the AR Emoji Studio.

- • AR Emoji Camera: To create your own Emoji avater use the camera.

- • Including augmented reality emoji stickers in your My Emoji avatar.

- • Adding line drawings or handwriting to your environment can improve movies. By tracking faces and space, AR Doodle can follow your motions.

- With the camera, you may instantly add embellishments to still photos or moving pictures.

- Quick measurement: Measure items in inches or millimeters using your camera.

Space Zoom

Capture up to 100 times-magnification, clear, and accurate pictures (Galaxy S23 Ultra only).

1. To select a magnification level, select Zoom from the shortcut menu under 📷 Camera.

- Center your subject in the frame, then tap Zoom lock to quickly and precisely focus the zoom while capturing photos at higher magnifications.

2. Videos made with Tap Capture Recordings

Record videos

Use your device to produce dynamic, flowing videos.

1. Swipe right or left to change between camera and video mode.

2. Press ⁎ Record to begin filming a video.

- Touch ⊙ Capture to snap a picture while you're filming.

- To briefly pause recording, tap ‖ Pause. To continue recording, select ⁎ Resume.

3. Tap ∎ Stop once you're done recording.

360 Audio recording

Use Bluetooth headphones and 360 audio recording to capture 3D audio that is immersive (sold separately).

1. From the 🔘 Camera menu, choose ⚙ Settings.

2. Click 360 audio recording under Advanced video options to turn it on.

Camera settings

Configure the camera with the icons on the camer

main screen.

- o Touch ⚙ Settings in the 📷 Camera menu to
  get to the following options:

Intelligence

- The scene optimizer automatically adjusts
  your photos' color settings to the scene.

- Get on-screen tips to help you line up great
  pictures. Shot recommendations

- Scan QR codes: The camera will seek for QR
  codes automatically.

Pictures

- You can select whether to take a burst of shots
  or create a GIF by swiping the shutter button
  to the edge that is closest to you.

- Place a watermark in the bottom left corner of
  each of your pictures.

- Advance photo options: choosing file formats and other storage options

  - Photos with high efficacy: Save pictures as high efficiency ones to reduce storage space. Not all sharing websites could be compatible with this format.

  - Image format in Pro mode: Choose the file type for photos saved in Pro mode.

Selfies

- Save selfie as previewed: You can store selfies as the show in the preview without flipping them.

Videos

- Auto FPS: This function automatically adjusts the frame rate in video mode to record videos that are more vivid in dim light.

- Switch on anti-shake in video stabilization to keep the focus when moving the camera.

- Advance video options: Improve your recordings by using modern recording formats.

- High-efficiency videos Use the HEVC format when recording videos to conserve space. It's possible that other devices or sharing websites won't be able to play this format.

- High-bitrate professional videos: Capture videos at a higher bit rate by using the Pro video shooting option.

- HDR10+ movies: Make HDR10+ recordings to improve videos. Playback devices must support HDR10+ video.

- Microphone with a zoom-in feature: While filming videos, sync the mic zoom with the camera zoom.

- 360 audio recording: Use your Bluetooth headphones to capture authentic, lifelike 3D sounds.

General

- Tracking auto-focus: Hold your attention on a moving target.

- Gridlines: Display gridlines in your viewfinder to help you compose your photos or videos.

- Give the films and photographs in your collection a GPS location tag.

- **Shooting strategies:**

  - The volume keys can be used to zoom, record videos, take images, and change the system volume.

  - Voice commands: While capturing pictures, say key phrases.

  - Floating shutter button: Add a second shutter button that can be moved across the screen.

  - Display palm: With your palm facing the camera, extend your hand to have your picture shot rapidly.

- Setting to keep: Select whether to launch Camera with the same photography mode, selfie angle, and filters as the previous launch.
- Shutter sound: Make a tone as soon as the camera shutters.
- Vibration feedback: Enable vibrations when you press the screen in the Camera app.

Privacy

- Privacy notice: See Samsung's privacy guidelines.
- Settings for permission: Under "Permissions," you can see the mandatory and discretionary permissions for the Camera app.

Other

- Reset settings: Reset the camera's settings.
- You can get in touch with us at: Through Samsung Members, contact Samsung support.
- Camera info: See details on the camera's software and applications.

 Gallery

Visit the Gallery to see all of the visual data that is kept on your device. Viewing, editing, and managing images and videos are all possible.

- o Tap  Gallery under the Applications section.

Viewing photo in gallery

You may see the photos on your device by using the Gallery app.

1. From the  Gallery menu, select Photos.

2. Tap a picture to view it. Swipe left or right to explore additional photos or videos.

- For the current image, tap ⊙ Bixby Vision to enable it. To learn more, consult Bixby.

- To include the image in your collection of favorites, tap ♡ Add to Favorites.

- To access the following features, click ⋮ More options:

  - Details: See and alter the info that goes with the image.

  - Re-mastering a photo means improving it with software-driven image corrections.

  - Add a portrait effect. You can adjust the background visibility in your portrait photos by using the slider.

  - Copies the image to the clipboard so that it can be pasted into another program.

  - Set as wallpaper: Set the picture as the backdrop of your computer.

  - Move to secure folder: Click the button to move the image to a safe location.

- Print: Send the picture to a local printer to print it.

Edit photos

To make your images better, use the editing tools in the Gallery.

1. Choose some images from the ✿ gallery.

2. To access the following options after seeing a photo, touch ✎ Edit.

- ☀ Auto adjustments: Apply adjustments to the image automatically.

- ⬚ Transform: Change the overall appearance of the image by rotating, flipping, cropping, or inputting other changes.

- ⬯ Filters: Use filters to add color effects.

- ☼ Tone: To change the brightness, exposure, contrast, and other characteristics of the tone, touch the icon.

- ☺ Decorations: Add text, stickers, or hand-drawn artwork as finishing touches.

- Touch more to get to more editing options.

- Revert: Reverting the modifications will restore the original image.

3. Tap Save when you're done.

Watch video

See what videos are on your smartphone. You can view the specifics of a video and add it to your favorites.

1. Click on Photos in the Gallery menu.

2. Tap on a video to start it playing. Swipe left or right to explore additional photos or videos.

- To include the video in your collection of favorites, tap Add to Favorites. The video is now accessible on the Favorites section of the Albums tab.

- To access the following features, tap More choices.

   - Details: Check out and edit the details about the video there.

- Open in video player: Launching the video player view this video using the integrated video player.

- Set as wallpaper: Make the background of the lock screen a video.

- Move to safe folder: Clicking the button will transfer this video to your Safe Folder.

3. To start the video, click ▶ Play.

Brighten Video

Select a setting by tapping Video brightness under ○ Advanced features in Settings to enhance the video's visual quality and enjoy more vivid and dynamic colors.

Video editing

On your device, arrange and edit videos.

1. From the ✳ Gallery menu, select Photos.

2. Tap on a video to start it playing.

3. Choose ✎ Edit to open the tools below:

- ◁)) Audio: Alter the background music and volume of the video.

- ▶ Play: A preview of the edited video can be viewed by clicking ▶ Play.

- ✂ Trim: Take away specific segments of the video.

- ⬚ Transform: Change the overall appearance of the video by rotating, flipping, cropping, or in any other way.

- ◌ Filters: With firlter you can add a beautiful visual effects to the video.

- ☼ Tone: Adjust the exposure, contrast, lighting, and other elements to alter the tone.

- ☺ Decorations: Add hand-drawn or text-based decorations to your work.

- ⋮ More: To access further editing capabilities, click ⋮ More.

- Revert: Reverting to the original version of the video means undoing the changes.

4. When prompted, click Confirm after choosing Save.

Share photo and videos

The Gallery app can be used to upload and share pictures and videos.

1. Tap ✽ Gallery, click images.

2. By choosing ⋮ More > Edit, choose the pictures or videos you want to share.

3. ⌁ Share: Choose the app or connection you wish to use to share your choice by clicking ⌁ Share and then choosing it. Follow the guidelines.

Delete the images and videos.

Remove any videos and pictures that are currently on your smartphone.

1. Under the ✽ Gallery, click **Edit** under ⋮ more options.

2. Touch the photos and videos you wish to select.

3. Click Yes when prompted, then choose Delete
🗑 .

Assemble similar photo

Images and videos in the Gallery can be sorted by similarity.

1. Click ✳ Group, touch ▱ Group similar images.

2. To return to the default Gallery layout, tap ▱ Ungroup.

Taking screenshot

Take a screen capture of your computer. The Gallery app on your smartphone will immediately create a Screenshots album.

o From any screen, hold down the Side and Volume Down buttons.

Swipe palm to take a screenshot

To take a picture of the screen, move your hand's edge across the surface while keeping contact with it.

1. Choose Palm swipe to capture from the
   Advanced features option in Settings.

2. Touch this icon 　 to activate this feature.

Screenshot settings

The screenshot settings can be modified.

○ Under Settings, choose Screenshots and
  screen recorder under 　 Advanced features.

- Show toolbar after capture: After taking a
  screenshot, present more options.

- Remove after sharing from toolbar: Use the
  screenshot toolbar to immediately delete
  screenshots after sharing them.

- Hiding the status and navigation bars: Making
  screenshots without the status or navigation
  bars visible.

- Format: Choose between JPG and PNG files to
  save your screenshots as.

- Save screeenshots: Choose a location to keep
  your screenshots when saving them.

Screen recorder

You can use your device to record videos of yourself to share with loved ones, track activities, and take notes.

1. Click Screen recorder in the Quick Settings section.

2. Tap Start recording after choosing a sound option.

3. There is a three-second countdown before the recording starts. To begin recording now, simply tap Skip countdown.

- Tap Draw to start drawing on the screen.

- To display an icon on the screen while using your S Pen, press Pointer (only works with the Galaxy S23 Ultra).

- To upload a clip from the front camera, select Selfie video.

4. Click ⬜ Stop to stop recording. They are frequently saved to the Gallery's album for screen recordings.

Screen recorder's settings

To change the screen recorder's sound and quality settings

- ○ Go to Settings > ◯ Advanced features > Screenshots and screen recorder.

- • Sound: Choose which sounds to record when using the screen recorder.

- • Make a decision regarding the video quality's resolution. Higher resolution and better quality options require more storage.

- • Selfie video duration: The slider can be used to change the size of the video overlay.

- • Display taps and touches: Enable the option to capture touches and taps on the screen.

- • Save screen recording: Choose a location for your screen recordings.

Using application

The Apps list displays all downloaded and installed programs. Users can download apps from the Google Play store and the Galaxy Store.

○ From the Home screen, swipe the screen upward to access the Apps list.

Disable or remove apps

You can remove installed programs from your device. Just disabling some preloaded (by default installed) applications is an option. Disabled applications are turned off and eliminated from the list of applications.

○ Under the Applications area, touch and hold an app to select Uninstall/Disable.

Search for apps

If you don't know where to seek for a particular program or configuration, use the Search tool.

1. Click Search in the list of apps, then enter one or more terms. When you type, corresponding

programs and settings are shown as search results.

2. Tap a result to launch an application.

Tips: you can modify your search preferences by selecting settings under ⋮ more options.

Sort apps

App shortcuts can be listed either alphabetically or in a particular order.

o Choose ⋮ More options > Sort from the Applications menu to see the following sorting options:

- Custom order: Manually organized app
- Alphabetical order: Sort apps alphabetically

Tips: When organizing programs manually, empty icon spaces can be removed by choosing ⋮ more choices > Clean up page.

Create and use folders

You can make folders on the Apps list to organize App shortcuts.

1. Slide an app shortcut over another app shortcut in Apps while touching and holding the first one to make it stand out.

2. Click the shortcut for the program to create the folder.

- Folder name: Name the folder by supplying a name for it.

- Palette: Change the folder's color using the palette.

- Add applications: Adding new programs to the folder After selecting the apps you want, tap Done.

3. Choose < Back to dismiss the folder.

Copy a folder to a Home screen

Copying a folder to the Home screen is possible.

o Tap and hold an app folder, then choose Add to Home.

Delete a folder

After deleting a folder, the program shortcuts are restored in the Apps list.

1. Touch and hold the folder in the Applications to delete it.

2. Choose 🗑 Delete folder when requested, then confirm.

Game Booster

Get better performance while playing games depending on your usage. Disable notifications and activate options to improve your gaming experience.

○ When playing a game, swipe up from the bottom of the screen to see the navigation bar. The following choices may be found on the far right and left sides:

• 📲Touch protection: Lock the display to prevent uninvited touching. This is the standard option.

- Booster for games: Set up extra options, including performance monitoring and blocking of menu bar, screen touches, and snapshots.

App settings

Manage the downloaded and installed apps.

- ○ Choose Apps under Settings. Choose an option to change:
- Select default apps: Choose the applications you wish to use for calling, messaging, browsing the web, and other activities.
- Samsung app settings: Seeing a list of the Samsung apps will allow you to adjust their settings.
- Your apps: Tap the app to see the privacy and usage options and make changes. Options vary depending on the app.

Tips: To restore previously changed app settings, choose More options > Reset app preferences.

Calendars

Set up accounts in the Calendar application.

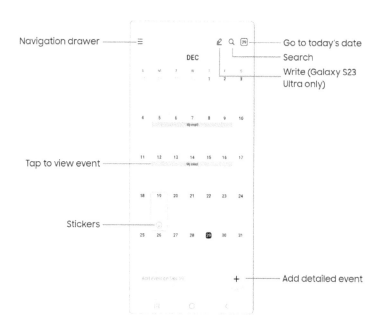

Navigation drawer ——— Go to today's date

Search

Write (Galaxy S23 Ultra only)

Tap to view event

Stickers

Add detailed event

Add calendars

You can set your accounts to the calendar app

1. After selecting Calendar, click Navigation drawer.

2. Under Manage calendars > Add account, select a kind of account.

3. Enter your account information and follow the on-screen directions.

TIP: Accounts may also have extra components like contacts and email.

Calendar alert style

The Calendar app allows users to choose from a variety of notification types.

1. From the 🔲 Calendar, select Alert style under ☰ Navigation drawer > ⚙ Calendar settings.

The options below are available:

- Light: Get an alert and a brief sound.
- Medium: A full-screen alert and a brief sound are audible.
- Strong: Get a full-screen alert with a persistent ringing noise until you ignore it.

2. Based on the alert style you previously selected, you have the following sound options:

- Short sound: Choose the alert sound for the Light or Medium alert types.

- Long sound: Choose the alert sound from the Strong alert sound options.

Create an event

Use your calendar to create events.

1. Choose 📅 Calendar > ✛ Add detailed event will allow you to add an event.

2. Complete the event's information, then tap **Save**.

Delete an event

Your Calendar can be cleared of events.

1. To change an event, tap it once in 📅 Calendar and then again.

2. When asked, click Yes after pressing the 🗑 Delete key.

⏰ Clock

Tools are available in the Clock app for tracking time and setting alarms.

Alarm in 43 minutes
Thu, Dec 29, 12:00 PM

Add alarm

6:00 AM · · · · · · · · · Turn alarm on or off

12:00 PM

5:00 PM

Alarm   World clock   Stopwatch   Timer

Alarm

Use the Alarm tab to set up one-time or repeating alerts and notification preferences.

1. Click ✛ Add alarm in the ◉ Clock section.
2. To set an alarm, tap one of the following:

*   Time: Choose an alarm time.
*   Day: Specify the alarm's daytime window.
*   Name the alarm: Give the alarm a name.
*   Alarm sound: Choose an alarm sound and use the slider to change the alarm's loudness.
*   Choose whether or not you want the alarm to vibrate as a warning.
*   Snooze: Permit going to sleep. While you are asleep, set the alarm's interval and repeat.

3. Click Save to save the alarm.

Tip: Tap ⋮ More options > to enter your sleep schedule, create a bedtime reminder, and quickly put your smartphone into sleep mode.

Remove an alarm

You can turn off an alarm you've set up.

1. Press and hold an alarm on the ⊙ clock.

2. Hit 🗑 Delete.

creating alerts

You can set the device to vibrate for alarms and timers regardless of whether the Sound mode is muted or set to vibrate.

1. Click Settings in the ⋮ More options section of the ⊙ Clock menu.

2. Choose the option Quiet alarms while system sound is off to turn it on.

Alarm setting

Notification for upcoming alert will display

1. While on ⊙ Clock click ⋮ More option> and then tap settings

2. Click upcoming alarm notification to select the number of minute before an upcoming alarm.

Chapter Four

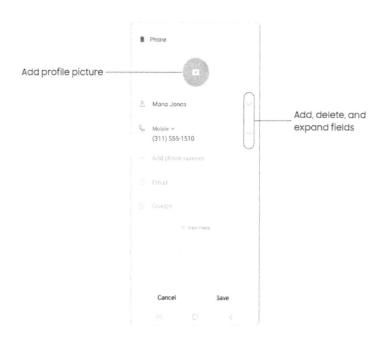Contacts

Organize and keep track of your contacts in contacts. You are able to sync personal accounts that you have added to your device. Calendars, email, and other services might also be supported by accounts.

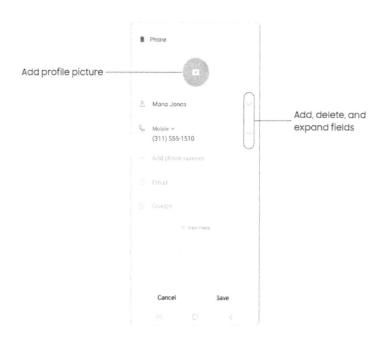

Add profile picture

Add, delete, and expand fields

Set up a contact

1. Click the ┼ Create contact option under the ⊖ Contacts menu.

2. Complete the contact's details, then click Save.

Modify the phone number

When editing a contact, you can tap a field to make changes to, add or remove data from, or add new fields to the contact's list of fields.

1. In ⊖ Contacts, first tap a contact.

2. Choose ⟋ Edit.

3. Touch any field to add, modify, or remove data.

4. Choose Save.

Favorites

People who have been added to your favorites list are displayed at the top of your contact list and are easy to find in other apps.

1. In ⊖ Contacts, first tap a contact.

2. Tap ☆ Favorites in step two to add a contact to your preferences.

    *   The contact can be deleted from your Favorites by tapping ☆ Favorites.

Transmit a contact

To spread a contact among others, make use of a number of services and sharing strategies.

1. In ⊖ Contacts, first tap a contact.

2. Press ⌁ Share.

3. Choose the Text or vCard file (VCF).

4. After choosing a sharing method, follow the directions.

Tip: Choose ⋮ More > QR code while seeing a contact to quickly share contact information with friends or family. The QR code is automatically updated when you make changes to the contact information boxes.

Show contacts while sharing contacts

You may share a phone number with your contacts app from any app with ease. Once activated, your frequently used contacts are displayed in the Sharing window.

o Click to activate the option, navigate to Settings > Advanced features > Display contacts when sharing content.

Groups

For managing your contacts, groups are a helpful tool.

Create a group.

Your personal contact lists should be built.

1. On the Contacts screen, select ☰ Display navigation menu > Groups.

2. Touch Create group, then tap fields to provide information for the group:

• Group name: The new group needs a name, so give it one.

- Group ringtone: Make the group's ringtone stand out by creating one.

- Adding members: Adding a member is as simple as selecting the contacts you wish to be a part of the new group and clicking Done.

3. Choose Save.

Remove or include group contacts

You can add or remove contacts from a group.

- From the 👤 Contacts menu, pick ☰ Display navigation menu > Groups, after which you should choose a group.

- Tap and hold to pick a contact, then press 🗑 Delete to delete it.

- Choose ✏ Edit > Add Member, then select the contacts you want to add. Choose Done > Save to preserve your work.

Group message sent

Send the group's members a text message.

1. Choose a group in 👤 Contacts by tapping ☰ Display navigation menu > Groups.

2. From the ⋮ More options menu, choose Send message.

To a group, send an email

Email group members to communicate.

1. Choose a group in 👤 Contacts by tapping ☰ Display navigation menu > Groups.

2. Choose Email under ⋮ More options.

3. Tap on the contacts you want to pick, or check the box at the top of the screen to select all of them, and then press Done.

- Only group participants whose records contain an email address are displayed.

4. Choose an email address and follow the guidelines.

Eliminate a group

Get rid of the group you created.

1. Choose a group in 😊 Contacts by tapping ☰ Display navigation menu > Groups.

2. From the More options menu, choose Erase group.

- To delete the group just, tap Delete group only.

- To delete the group and the contacts inside of it, tap Delete group and select Move members to trash.

Command contacts

Contacts can be exported or imported, and they can be joined into a single contact record.

Connect contacts

You can merge contact information from various sources into one contact by connecting entries into one contact.

1. In the 😊 Contacts app, select Manage contacts from the ☰ Show navigation menu menu.

2. Choose "Merge contacts." Duplicate contact information, including names, email addresses, and phone numbers, will be listed together.

3. After tapping to pick all of the contacts, click Merge.

contact import

Your device may import contacts as vCard files (VCF).

1. In the 🕴Contacts app, select Manage contacts from the ≡ Show navigation menu menu.

2. Choose Import contacts and follow the directions.

Contacts for export

Export contacts from your smartphone as vCard files (VCF).

1. Choose Manage contacts under ☰ Display navigation menu under the 👤 Contacts menu.

2. Choose Export contacts and follow the on-screen directions.

Contact sync

On each and every one of your accounts, update the contact information.

1. Choose Manage contacts under ☰ Display navigation menu under the 👤 Contacts menu.

2. Next select Contacts Sync.

Delete contact

Remove multiple or single contacts.

1. Press and hold a contact to select it in the 👤 Contact menu.

- From the deletion menu, you can also press other contact to select them.

2. Tap 🗑 Delete, and confirm when prompted

Remove contact

One or more contacts may be taken out at once.

1. In the 👤 Contacts app, touch and hold a contact to choose it for deletion.

- You can tap other contacts to pick them as well.

2. Choose 🗑 Delete when requested, then click the confirm button.

Emergency contact

You can still make calls to your emergency contacts if your smartphone is locked.

o Choose 🔒 Emergency contacts from the Settings menu under Safety and emergencies.

- Put members: Your emergency contacts will be determined by contacts you choose from your phone.
- Show on lock screen: The lock screen displays emergency contact information for quick access.

Phone

Look into the advanced calling features to see what more the Phone app can do than making calls. Speak with your service provider to learn more. The actual appearance of the Phone app interface and the available options vary by service provider.

Access voicemail

Make a video call

Make a call

Calls

The Phone app allows you to make and receive calls from the Home screen, Recents tab, Contacts, and other places.

Create a call

The Home screen of your phone can be used to make and receive calls.

- o Type a phone number into the keypad and choose Call from Phone app.
- • Tap Keypad to reveal the keypad if it is hidden.

Call someone from Recent Calls

Each call, both incoming and outgoing, is recorded in the call log.

1. On the Phone app, select Recents to view a list of recent calls.

2. Choosing a contact will prompt you to tap Call.

Call someone by using Contacts.

Make a call to a contact using the Contacts app.

o Swipe your finger across a contact's name to the right to call them from the Contacts app.

Receive a call

As a call comes in, the phone rings and the name or number of the caller is displayed. If you're utilizing an app, a pop-up call screen will show up.

o To answer the call, drag Answer to the right on the incoming call screen.

TIP: On the screen that appears when an incoming call comes in, tap Answer to accept it.

Reject the call.

You can decide whether to ignore an incoming call. If you're utilizing an app, a pop-up call screen will show up.

- o On the incoming call screen, drag Decline to the left to reject the call and send it to voicemail.

TIP: Choose Refuse a call on the incoming pop-up screen by tapping Decline and send it to voicemail.

Reject with a message

Drag Send a message upward and choose a message from the screen that appears when an incoming call comes in to reject the call by sending a text message in return.

- o On the screen that pops up when a call comes in, pull a message upward and select a message.

Tip: Tap send message and select a message on the incoming call pop-up menu.

Refuse a call

Tap 🔘 End call when you're prepared to hang up the phone.

When on a call, do this

You can perform other things, change to a headset or speaker, and adjust the call volume while on a call.

 o Press the Volume keys to change the volume.

Set the speaker or the headset to on.

To hear the call, utilize a Bluetooth® headset or the speakerphone (not included).

 o Choose ⚡ Bluetooth or 🔊 Speaker, based on whether you want to hear the caller through a Bluetooth headset or the speaker.

Multitask

If you switch to another app while in the call screen, your active call will be visible in the Status bar.

To go back to the call screen:

- o Tap the call to return to the call screen after dragging the Status bar to reveal the Notification panel.

To end a call while multitasking:

Drag the Status bar up to access the Notification panel while multitasking, press ⬤ End call, and then drag it back down to end the call.

Call background

Choose a picture or a video to play each time you make or receive a call.

- o Choose ⋮ More options > Settings > Call background on the ⓒ Phone to see the following options:

- **Layout**: You have the option of displaying a caller's profile photo when one is available.

- **Background**: This feature allows you to pick a picture to to display during a call.

Pop-up menu for incoming calls

When calls are made while using other programs, they may display as pop-up windows.

o Choose Call display while using applications under More ⋮ options > Settings > 🅲 Phone menu. The option below are available:

- **Full-screen**: Full-screen allows an incoming call to show in full.

- **Small pop-up:** Put a tiny pop-up alerting the user of an incoming call at the top of the screen.

- **Mini pop-up:** When an incoming call comes in, display a smaller pop-up.

- **Keep calls in pop-up:** By selecting this option, calls will remain in the pop-up window even after being answered.

Manage calls

Every call you make is recorded in a call log. Voicemail, blocking of numbers, and setting up speed dials are all options.

Call log

The phone numbers of the calls you have placed, received, or missed are listed in the call log.

o   On the screen of the 🅒 Phone app, select Recents. It displays a list of the most recent calls. If the caller is in your list of contacts, their name will show up.

Save a contact from recent call list

Using information from recent calls, make a new contact or edit the one you already have.

1. Click Recents in the 🅒 Phone app's menu.
2. After tapping the call containing the information you want to save, choose Add to contacts from the menu.
3. Choose either Create New Contact or Update Existing Contact.

Erase call history

To eliminate Call log entries:

1. From the 🅒 phone, select Recents.

2. To delete a call from the Call log, touch and hold the call.

3. Click 🗑 Delete a Phone Number.

Block a number

When a caller is added to your Block list, all incoming calls from that number will be routed to voicemail rather than being answered.

1. From the 🅒 phone, select Recents.

2. Touch the caller whose number you wish to add to the Block list, then press ⓘ Details.

3. Click OK when prompted, then choose 🚫 Block or ⋮ More > Block contact.

TIP: Your Block list can be modified in Settings. Choose Block numbers from the Phone Speed Dial from the More options menu.

Speed dial

You can provide a shortcut number to your contacts so they can quickly dial their default number.

1. On the 🅒 Phone screen, select Fast dial from the Keypad > ⋮ More options > menu.

2. Choose any number and press it.

- Number 1 is reserved for voicemail

- Press ▼ Menu to select a new Speed dial number from the list's following entry.

3. Type a name or phone number, or choose 👤 Add from Contacts to link the number to an existing contact.

- The chosen contact can be seen in the speed dial number field.

Make a call with speed dial

You can dial a number using Speed dial.

○ Go to 🅒 Phone and then Touch and hold the speed dial number.

- Enter the first few digits and then hold the last digit if the speed dial number contains more than one digit.

Remove a speed dial number

You can remove a Speed dial number you set.

1. On the 🄲 Phone app screen, click Fast dial under ⋮ more options.

2. To remove a contact from your speed dial, tap ⚊ Delete next to that contact.

Emergency calls

You can dial the local emergency number whether or not your phone is working. If your phone isn't turned on, the only call you can make is an emergency call.

1. On the 🄲 Phone app, call the appropriate emergency number (911 in North America).

2. Wrap up your call. During this type of call, you get access to the majority of in-call features.

TIP: By dialing the emergency number, anyone can use your phone to call for help if they need it even if it is locked. When accessed from a locked screen, only the emergency calling capability is available to the caller. The phone is still locked on the rest of it.

Phone settings

These options allow you to modify settings for the Phone app.

- Choose Settings from ⋮ more options on the 🌀 phone.

Optional calling services

Your wireless service provider and service package might support the following calling services.

Place a multi-party call

Make another call while speaking with someone on the phone. Options may vary per service provider.

1. To make the second call, choose ＋ Add call from the current call's menu.

2. Type in the new number and choose 📞 Call. After the call is answered:

- Switch between the two calls by tapping the On Hold number or the Tap⬜ Switch button.
- To hear both callers at once, select ⤳ Merge (multi-conferencing)

Video calls

To engage in video calls

○ Choose ▇ Meet or ▇ Video Call, or ○ Video Call after dialing a number.

NOTE: Not every device can do video calls. The caller has the option of answering the call using a standard voice call or accepting the video call.

Effects for video call

You can blur or change your background during a video conference using the various apps.

1. In the Settings menu, choose Video call effects under ○ Advanced features

2. To activate this feature, tap ◗

3. Choose a pick from the options:

131

- Background color: Adapt your virtual background to your surroundings by choosing a solid color.

- Background image: To use as the background of your video conference, pick a photo from your collection.

Wi-Fi calling

Calls can be placed over Wi-Fi while you are connected to a Wi-Fi network.

1. From the Phone app, select More choices > Settings > Wi-Fi calling.

2. To activate this feature, tap

3. Adhere to the Wi-Fi calling setup and configuration instructions.

Real Time Text (RTT)

You can type with the other person in real-time while you are on a call.

RTT is available whenever you dial a phone that supports RTT or is linked to a teletypewriter (TTY) device. The RTT indicator appears on each incoming RTT call.

1. From the 📞 Phone app, choose ⋮ More options > Settings.

2. To access the following options, select Real time text.

- RTT call button: Set the visibility of the RTT call button.

  - Only shown during calls: Only when a call is in progress will the RTT call button appear.

  - Always visible: The RTT call button should be visible on the keypad and during calls.

- Use a TTY external keyboard: The RTT keyboard should be hidden when an external TTY keyboard is connected.

- TTY mode: Choose the best TTY configuration for the currently-used keyboard.

Messages

By sending quick greetings, emoticons, and images to your contact, you may remain in touch with them using the Messages app. Options may vary per service provider.

- o Click ○ Compose new message in the 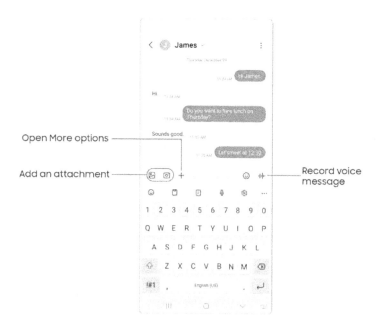 Message app.

Search for message

To easily locate a message, use the search tool.

1. From the ⊙ Messages menu, select ⌕ Search.

2. Enter a few search terms in the field provided, then press the ⌕ Search key on the keyboard.

Delete conversation

Your conversion history can be erased by deleting chats.

1. Under ⋮ More options, select 🗑 Delete under Messages.

2. Tap the chats you want to delete.

3. Click Yes when prompted after selecting 🗑 Remove all.

Emergency message

Send an audio and visual message to your emergency contacts.

- ○ Choose 🔔 Emergency SOS under Safety and emergencies in the Settings menu. You can start the following processes by pressing the Side key five times:
- • Countdown: Choose the number of seconds that will pass before emergency actions are initiated.
- • Make emergency call: Dial the appropriate number to place an emergency call.
- • Share info with emergency contacts: Emergency contacts might request your whereabouts if you share information with them.

TIP: You can activate Emergency SOS while choosing 📞 Emergency Call by pressing and holding the Side and Volume Down keys at the same time.

Sharing in emergency

Send an audio and visual message to your emergency contacts.

1. Click Emergency sharing under ⬛ Safety and emergencies in the Settings menu. Decide what to send to your emergency contacts if you feel the need for assistance:

- Add pictures: Your front and back cameras are for taking and sending pictures.

- Add audio record: Transmit the five-second audio file that is attached.

2. Tap Start emergency sharing to share the selected media with your emergency contacts.

Message settings

Make it possible to send text and multimedia messages.

o Choose Settings under ⋮ Additional choices in 💬 Messages app

137

Notification of emergency

Emergency alerts will notify you of impending threats and other crises. It costs nothing to get an emergency alert.

- o Choose Wireless Emergency Alerts under Settings > Safety and emergency to customize alert alerts.

TIP: Notifications also provides access to emergency alerts. The Notifications > Advanced settings > Wireless Emergency Alerts menu option can be found under Settings.

Internet

A simple, quick, and reliable web browser for your device is Samsung Internet. Find out about additional secure web browsing features that will enhance your browsing experience and make it faster and more private.

Hardware and software are constantly evolving, therefore the images you see here are only meant as a point of reference.

Browser tabs

Use tabs to see several websites simultaneously.

- o Choose New Tab > 🟢 Internet from the 1️⃣ Tabs menu.

- • Touch 1️⃣ > ❌ Close tab. The tab will close

Add a bookmark

Create bookmarks for your favorite websites to access them fast.

1. Click ⭐ Add to favorites from 🟢 Internet to add the currently viewed webpage.

Launch a bookmark

Use the Bookmarks page to instantly launch a webpage.

1. Choose ⭐ Bookmarks under 🟢 Internet.
2. Choose a bookmark listing.

Save a website

A webpage can be saved in a variety of ways using the Samsung Internet app.

o To access the following options, select ☰

   Tools > Add page to from 🔵 Internet.

- Bookmarks: Save the webpage to your list of Favorites using bookmarks.

- Quick access: See a list of commonly used or saved websites for easy access.

- Home screen: Create a shortcut to the webpage and place it there.

- Saved pages: By storing a webpage to your device, you can access it while you are not connected to the internet.

See history

A list of recently visited websites can be viewed by

selecting ☰ Tools > History from the 🔵 Internet.

TIP: Choose ⋮ More choices. Delete history to get rid of your surfing data

Sharing pages

Websites can be shared with friends and acquaintances.

- Choose ☰ Tools > Share from ⊙ Internet and then follow the on-screen instructions.

Secret mode

Sites seen in Secret mode don't show up in your search history or browser history, and they don't leave any traces (like cookies) on your computer. Compared to standard tab windows, secret tabs are a distinct color.

Any downloaded files are still available on your device even after you close the secret tab.

1. Click ⬜ Tabs > Enable secret mode from ⊙ internet app.

2. To open the browser in Secret mode, press Start.

Secret mode settings

A password or biometric lock is necessary to use Secret mode.

1. Click 🔲 Tabs in the 🔵 Internet menu.

2. Choose the ensuing choices by clicking ⋮ Additional options > Secret mode settings:

   • Use password: Create a password in order to activate Secret mode and use biometrics.

   • Reset secret mode: Reset your Secret mode settings and remove all of your data.

Deactivate Secret mode

To return to standard browsing, turn off Secret mode.

   ○ On 🔵 Internet app, click 🔲 tab> turn off secret mode.

Internet settings

The options for the settings of the Internet app are editable.

   ○ Click ☰ Tools > Settings after opening 🔵 Internet.

 **My Files**

See and arrange the images, videos, songs, and audio clips that are saved on your device. In addition, you have control over and access to the data kept in your cloud accounts.

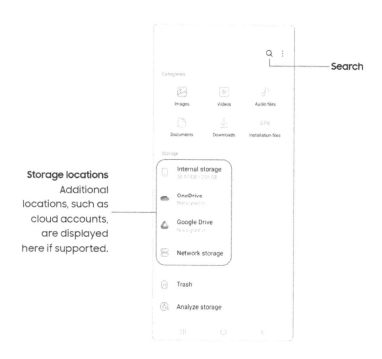

Search

Storage locations
Additional locations, such as cloud accounts, are displayed here if supported.

Group files

To organize the files on the device, the following categories are used:

- Latest files: Choose Recent Files to view recently viewed files.

- This choice is displayed only if one or more files have recently been visited.

- Categories: Browse your files by category to find the right one.

- Storage: Access information kept both on your machine and on the cloud.

- Your cloud accounts alter based on which services you log into.

- Analyze storage: Go through your storage to see what is using up space there.

My Files Settings

Use the My Files settings to modify your file management choices and more. Options may vary per service provider.

o From My Files, select More options > Settings to access the options listed below:

145

- Cloud accounts: By entering into your cloud accounts, you may manage your cloud services.

- File management: File management gives you control over how to utilize, erase, and display mobile data for files.

- Analyze storage: While analyzing storage, choose a file size to emphasize.

- Privacy: Verify the permissions for My Files under "Privacy."

Samsung Health

Make use of Samsung Health to plan and keep track of a variety of daily activities that have an impact on wellbeing, such as exercise, nutrition, and sleep.

NOTE: The information gathered by this device, Samsung Health, or related software is not intended for use in making medical diagnoses or in the treatment, mitigation, or prevention of illness.

The environment in which the device is used, a specific activity performed while wearing it, the device's settings, user configuration/information supplied by the user, and other end-user interactions can all affect how accurate the data and information provided by this device and its associated software are.

Before you start working out

It's always essential to consult with your doctor before beginning any workout regimen, even though the Samsung Health app is an excellent fitness partner. Even though the majority of people can safely engage in moderate exercise, such as brisk walking, health experts advise speaking with your doctor before starting an exercise program, especially if you have any of the following conditions: heart disease, asthma, lung disease, diabetes, liver disease, kidney disease, or arthritis.

Before beginning an exercise regimen, speak with your doctor if you experience any signs of a serious condition, such as pain or discomfort in your arms, neck, jaw, chest, or during physical activity.

- Swelling of the ankles, especially at night; Lightheadedness or unconsciousness;
- Muscular discomfort that goes away after resting when descending stairs or ascending a hill
- Shortness of breath with minimal exercise or at rest;

It is suggested that you see a medical expert before beginning an exercise regimen. If you are pregnant, have a variety of health conditions, or are unclear of your health situation, speak with your doctor before starting a new fitness program.

![icon] Samsung Notes

Using social networking platforms, sharing your notes is easy when you use Samsung Notes to create notes with text, footnoted photos, voice recordings, and music.

149

Make a note

Include text, images, audio files, and other types of media.

1. First, select Add in Samsung Notes.

2. When creating content, use the text-based options.

Voice recording

Make voice memos with annotations that are perfect for seminars or meetings, and record audio as you take notes. The playback is synchronized with the scrolling of the text.

1. Choose Add in Samsung Notes.

2. From the Tap Insert menu, choose Voice recording.

3. Write something while the audio is being recorded by utilizing the text options.

Edit notes

Modify the notes that you make.

1. To view a note in Samsung Notes, tap

2. To change something, tap ✎ Edit.

3. Choose ⟨ Navigate up after you're finished.

Option for notes

It is possible to organize, sort, or edit notes.

o In Samsung Note, The following substitutes are available:

- ⬚+ Import PDF: To import a PDF file into Samsung Notes, open it.

- 🔍 Search: Look up a word or phrase.

- ⋮ More

- Edit: Choose which notes you want to move, share, get rid of, save as a file, or lock.

- View: Choose either the Grid, List, or Simple list view.

- Top-pin your preferred items: Keep the notes you've marked as favorites at the top of the main page.

Note menu

By category, you can access your notes.

- ○ To access the following options, tap ☰ Show navigation menu in 🅾Samsung Notes.

- Settings: You may access the Samsung Notes app's settings here.

- All notes: See all notes.

- Shared notebooks: Log in to your Samsung account to see shared notebooks that you have with your connections.

- Trash: See deleted notes for up to 15 days in the trash.

- Folders: Folders are used to organize notes.

- Manage folders: Add, remove, and rearrange folders.

Access settings

There are several ways to get to your device's settings.

- Choose ⚙ Settings by swiping down from the Home screen.

- Click ⚙ Settings in the Applications menu.

Find a settings

If you aren't sure where a setting is, you can search for it.

1. To start a search, select 🔍 Search from the Settings menu.

2. Tap a selection to open a setting.

Chapter Five

Connections

With the help of Connections Wi-Fi, you may control the connections between your device and other networks and other devices.

Wi-Fi

You can access the Internet by connecting your device to a Wi-Fi network without using your mobile data.

1. Select Connections > Wi-Fi in the Settings menu, then tap to activate Wi-Fi and look for open networks.

2. Tap a network, and if a password prompt appears, type it in.

3. Choose Connect.

Connect to a hidden Wi-Fi network

If, following a scan, the Wi-Fi network you're looking for is not found, you can still connect to it by manually entering the information. Ask the WiFi network administrator for the name and password before you begin.

1. Click Connections > Wi-Fi in the Settings menu, then click to turn on Wi-Fi.

2. Click Add network at the bottom of the list.

3. Provide information about the WiFi network:

- Network name: Put the complete name of the network here.

- Security: Choose a level of security from the list, and if required, enter the password.

- Password: Put the network password in the Password field.

- Hidden network: There should be a covert network.

- See more: Add more complex parameters, such as IP and proxy settings.

4. Choose Save.

TIP: To connect to a Wi-Fi network, use the camera on your device to scan a ▦ QR code.

Direct Wi-Fi Direct

Devices can transport data over Wi-Fi with Wireless

1. Click 🛜 Connections > Wi-Fi in the Settings menu, then click ⚏ to turn on Wi-Fi.

2. From the ⋮ Additional options section, pick Wi-Fi Direct.

3. Tap a device, then follow the connection instructions.

Disconnect from Wi-Fi Direct

Remove your gadget from a Wi-Fi Direct network.

o Go to Settings and choose 🛜 Connections > Wi-Fi > ⋮ More to access Wi-Fi Direct. Tap the device to unplug it.

Intelligent Wi-Fi settings

You may manage saved networks, verify the network addresses of your device, and set up connections to different Wi-Fi network and hotspot types. Options may vary per service provider.

1. Click Connections > Wi-Fi in the Settings menu, then click to turn on Wi-Fi.

2. To access the following options, select Intelligent Wi-Fi under ⁝ Additional options:

- Turn mobile data: Whenever the Wi-Fi connection is unstable when enabled, your device will switch to mobile data. When a strong Wi-Fi signal is present, it switches back to Wi-Fi.

- Switch to stronger Wi-Fi networks: Switch to faster or more dependable Wi-Fi networks: automatically switch to Wi-Fi networks with these improvements.

- Automatic Wi-Fi on/off: Activate Wi-Fi in locations that are frequently visited.

- Display network quality info: On the list of accessible Wi-Fi networks, display network details (such as speed and dependability).

157

- Priotize real-time data: Lag-sensitive tasks like video calls and games should be given this treatment.

- Detect problematic networks: Get notifications when the active Wi-Fi network behaves suspiciously.

- Wi-Fi power saving mode: To prolong battery life, turn on Wi-Fi traffic analysis in the power-saving mode.

- Automatic Hotspot Connection: When a Wi-Fi hotspot is discovered, automatically connect to it.

- Intelligent Wi-Fi: View the website in Intelligent Wi-Fi mode.

Advanced Wi-Fi settings

You may manage saved networks, verify the network addresses of your device, and set up connections to different Wi-Fi network and hotspot types. Options may vary per service provider.

1. Click 🛜 Connections > Wi-Fi in the Settings menu, then click ⬤ to turn on Wi-Fi.

2. Choose the ⋮ More option>Advanced setting to see the following options:

- Sync with Samsung Cloud/account: Wi-Fi profiles will be synchronized with your Samsung account via the Samsung cloud.

- Show Wi-Fi pop-up: Alert me when opening apps to the presence of Wi-Fi.

- Wi-Fi notification: Get updates when open networks are discovered nearby using network notifications and Wi-Fi notifications.

- Manage networks: Browse your saved Wi-Fi networks and decide which ones you wish to auto-reconnect to or forget.

- On/off Wi-Fi history: See which applications most recently turned your Wi-Fi on or off.

- Hotspot 2.0: With Hotspot 2.0, you can automatically connect to Wi-Fi networks that support it.

- Install network certificates: Install authentication certificates after network certificates are installed.

Bluetooth

Your device can be associated with other Bluetooth-capable devices, such as Bluetooth headphones or a Bluetooth-enabled car entertainment system. As soon as a pairing is completed, the devices remember one another and can interact without having to enter the passkey again.

1. Choose Bluetooth from the Connections > Settings menu, and then select it.

2. Tap a device, then follow the connecting instructions that appear.

TIP: Tap the file you want to share before using Bluetooth. Click Bluetooth.

Rename a paired device

You can alter the name of a connected device to make it easier to recall.

1. Choose Bluetooth from the Connections > Settings menu, and then select it.

2. Next to the device name after choosing Settings, choose **Rename**.

3. Enter a new name, then click **Rename**

Unpair from a Bluetooth device

When you unpair from a Bluetooth device, the two devices are no longer recognized by one another, therefore you have to pair with the device again in order to connect to it.

1. Choose Bluetooth from the Connections > Settings menu, and then select it.

2. Choose Settings next to the device, then select Unpair.

3. Choose "Un-pair" to confirm.

Advanced Bluetooth settings

More Bluetooth options are available in the Advanced menu. Options may vary per service provider.

1. Choose Bluetooth under connections in the Settings menu.

2. Click on Advanced settings or Additional options to open the following menus. Other settings:

• Sync with Samsung cloud/account: Files sent over Bluetooth can be synced with your Samsung account or the Samsung Cloud.

• Music Sharing: Enable your Bluetooth speaker or headphones so that friends can listen to music.

• Ringtone sync: When a Bluetooth device is linked, you can utilize the ringtone that is pre-programmed on your device to answer calls.

- Bluetooth control history: The Bluetooth control history feature allows you to view the most recent Bluetooth activity by apps.

- Block pairing requests: Block pairing requests by include the desired devices in the list.

- Bluetooth scan history: Using Bluetooth scan history, you can see which apps have recently looked for nearby Bluetooth devices and use those apps' Bluetooth features.

Dual audio

Your device's audio can be received by two associated Bluetooth audio devices.

1. Start by connecting your device to Bluetooth audio equipment.

2. Click the Notification panel's Media output button.

3. To play audio to each audio device, tap the icon next to it in the Audio output section (up to two devices).

NFC and payment

Near field communication allows you to talk to another device without utilizing a network (NFC). Several payment apps, such as Android Beam, both utilize this ability. The sending device must have NFC capabilities, and the receiving device must be four centimeters away.

- o Tap NFC and contactless payments under Connections in Settings to make this feature active.

Pay and Tap

You can make purchases by putting your phone near an NFC-enabled credit card reader.

1. Open Settings, then tap NFC and contactless payments under Connections to enable NFC. To activate this feature tap

2. Choose Contactless payments in order to see the default payment app.

- If you want to use a different payment app, tap one of the options to choose it.

- To utilize a payment app that is already open, click Pay with currently open app.

- The selected payment service can then be chosen to become the default by selecting Others.

Ultra-wideband

Determine the closest devices' precise position. Options may vary per service provider.

○ Choose Ultra-wideband under Settings > Connections to enable this capability (UWB).

Airplane mode

When the phone is in airplane mode, all network connections, including mobile data, Wi-Fi, Bluetooth, and talking and texting, are turned off. When Airplane mode is on, you can activate Wi-Fi and Bluetooth in Settings or from the Quick settings window.

- Choose Connections from the Settings menu, then tap Airplane mode to enable this feature.

NOTE: Using mobile devices while traveling by ship or airplane may be subject to federal and local rules and restrictions. When in airplane mode, none of the network access will be available. Although it is not permitted on board cars or ships, ultra-wideband (UWB) can be turned off by using the Airplane mode. Consult the right authorities regarding the proper hours and methods to use your gadget, and always follow crew instructions.

SIM management

Your cellular service provider and service plan may allow you to use a dual SIM (two physical SIM cards) or an eSIM in order to manage two mobile accounts without carrying two devices (embedded SIM). Options may vary per service provider.

Devices with dual SIM capabilities have two SIM card slots. It might also have a microSD card slot for further storage, if supported. Upon launch, dual SIM-capable devices will get software updates that make the built-in feature functional.

A genuine SIM card is not required for the operation of devices that support an eSIM. Due of this, voice, text, and data can be used with either the eSIM or a regular SIM card. Following launch, devices that support eSIM will receive software upgrades that enable the integrated eSIM capabilities.

To access the following option, go to Settings > Connections > SIM management.

- SIM cards: You can alter the names of the actual SIM cards that are already installed in your smartphone or view them.

- eSIMs: Choose ✛ Add eSIM to add a current eSIM mobile plan or to create a new one.

- Main SIM: Choose one SIM card to be the main one, which will be used for calls, messages, and data if you have more than one.

167

- More SIM settings: Tap to learn about additional SIM card management choices.

Mobile networks

Using mobile networks, you may configure your device to connect to them and gain access to mobile data. Options may vary per service provider.

- On the Settings menu, select ⦿ Connections > Mobile networks.
- Mobile data: Permit using mobile data.
- International data roaming: For foreign roaming, voice, text, and data roaming options can be modified.
- Data roaming access: While roaming for data, configure access to mobile networks.
- Data roaming: Permit the use of data when moving between mobile networks.
- Enhanced Calling: For improved communication, use LTE data.
- System select: If your service provider allows it, change the CDMA roaming mode.

- Access point name: Access Point Names (APNs) are the network configurations required for your device to connect to your provider; you may add or change APNs here.

- Network operation: Choose your preferred networks from those that are offered.

- Mobile network diagnostic: For troubleshooting, compile usage and diagnostic data.

- Network extenders: You should search for cells that can strengthen your network connection

TIP: Use these settings to help you manage connection parameters that could affect your monthly bill.

Use of date

Check your current Wi-Fi and mobile data usage. Also customizable are the limitations and warnings.

o Tap Connections > Data use in the Settings menu.

Switch on data saving

Data Saver helps reduce the amount of data you use by preventing certain apps from sending or receiving data in the background.

1. Select Settings > Connections > Data use > Data saver.

2. Activate Data Saver on by tapping

- When Data Saver is turned on, select Allow use of data. If you wish to allow some apps to consume limitless data, tap next to each app to establish limitations.

Check mobile data

You may limit how your mobile data is accessed by placing restrictions and controls in place. Options may vary per service provider.

- On the Settings menu, select Connections > Data use. The options below are available:

- Mobile data: When travelling abroad, mobile data services ought to be turned on.

- International data roaming: Even when your device is linked to Wi-Fi, set up apps to constantly use mobile data.

- Mobile data only apps: Using mobile data Monitor the amount of data utilized while a mobile device is connected over time.

- Mobile data usage: Overall consumption and usage by individual apps.

- Billing cycle and data warning: Change the monthly date to match the date your service provider specifies for invoicing.

Tip: Take advantage of these capabilities to keep an eye on your anticipated data usage.

Monitor Wi-Fi data

You can restrict Wi-Fi data access by configuring use caps and networks to your preferences.

1. Choose Settings > Connections > Data use.
2. Tap Wi-Fi data usage in step two to track Wi-Fi data usage over a period of time. There are

171

two options: overall consumption and usage by individual apps.

Mobile hotspot

With a mobile hotspot, your data plan becomes a Wi-Fi network that numerous devices can join.

1. Choose Mobile hotspot from the Settings menu under Connections > Mobile hotspot and tethering.

2. Touch to switch on Mobile hotspot.

3. Choose your mobile hotspot choice after turning on Wi-Fi on the desired connected devices. The mobile hotspot password must be entered to connect.

Tip: When adding a new device to your mobile hotspot, scan the QR code instead of entering the password.

Configure mobile hotspot settings

Your mobile hotspot's connectivity and security settings are modifiable.

1. Choose Mobile hotspot from the Settings menu under 📶 Connections > Mobile hotspot and tethering.

2. Choose Configure to reveal the following settings:

- Network name: See and change your mobile hotspot's name under "Network name."

- Password: If you choose a security level that demands one, you can view or modify your password.

- Bandwidth: Choose a bandwidth option from the list provided.

- Security: Choose your mobile hotspot's security level under "Security".

- Advanced: Put up additional mobile hotspot preferences in the advanced mode.

Auto hotspot

sharing your hotspot connection with extra devices that have automated Samsung account logins.

1. Choose Mobile hotspot from the Settings menu under 🛜 Connections > Mobile hotspot and tethering.

2. Choose Auto hotspot, and then press ▶ to make the feature active.

Tethering

You can tether devices to share your Internet connection with another device. Options may vary per service provider.

1. Under the Settings section, select 🛜 Connections > Mobile hotspot and tethering.

2. Decide from the following options:

• Choose Bluetooth tethering to use Bluetooth to share your Internet connection

• Choose USB tethering after connecting the device and PC using a USB connection

• Enable Ethernet tethering after using an Ethernet adapter to join the computer to the gadget.

174

Scanning for nearby devices

Connections to other accessible devices can be easily created by turning on Nearby device scanning. This tool alerts you when there are devices available to connect to.

1. Choose Nearby device scanning under Connections > Additional connection settings in the Settings menu

2. Touch to make the feature active.

Ethernet

If a wireless network connection is not available, an Ethernet cable can be used to connect your device to a local network.

1. Connect your equipment via an Ethernet wire.

2. From the Settings menu, select Connections > Additional connection settings > Ethernet. Then, follow the on-screen prompts.

TIP: An adaptor is required to connect an Ethernet wire to your device (which is not supplied).

Network lock status

To see if it can be unlocked for use on another mobile network, check the state of your device's network lock. Options may vary per service provider.

- o   Touch Network lock status under Additional connection settings in the Settings menu.

Connected gadgets

Consolidate mobile connectivity between your handset and other connected devices.

- o   Choose connected devices from Settings to access the following features.
- •   Quick Share: makes it possible for anyone with a Samsung account to share files with your device.
- •   Auto switch Buds: Your Galaxy Buds will automatically switch from another device to

this one whenever you place or receive a call or play media.

- Call and text from other devices: To make and receive calls and text messages, use your Galaxy devices that are signed into your Samsung account.

- Continue applications on other devices: Continue using the apps you were using earlier on your Galaxy devices that are logged into your Samsung account.

- Link to Windows: Connect your device to a Windows PC to have rapid access to the photos, messages, and other stuff on it.

- Multiple controls: On your Galaxy Book, use the keyboard and cursor to move things back and forth.

- Samsung DeX: Connect your device to a PC or TV for a better multitasking experience.

- Smart View: Allows you to show the screen of your device or stream videos to a nearby TV.

- Galaxy wearable: The Galaxy Wearable function on your phone lets you connect it to your Samsung watch and earbuds.

- SmartThings: Use SmartThings to connect your device to a network of smarter living options.

- Android auto: In order to focus on driving, connect your device to any compatible car display using Android Auto.

Sound and Vibration

You have control over the sounds and vibrations that are used to indicate screen taps, notifications, and other interactions.

sound mode

You don't need to adjust the level to change the sound mode on your device.

- Choosing a mode is done by tapping Sounds and vibration in the Settings section.

- Sound: The sounds, vibrations, and volume levels that you have chosen in the Sound settings will be used for notifications and alerts.

   - Vibrate in addition to ringing: When you receive a call, configure your smartphone to vibrate in addition to ringing.

- Vibrate: Vibration should only be used for alerts and notifications.

- Mute: Disable all audio output from your device.

   - Temporary mute: Set a time limit for the device's mute state.

Tip: Use the sound mode setting instead of the volume buttons to change the sound mode without erasing your personalized sound settings.

Mute with hand gestures

To instantly suppress sounds, cover the phone's screen or turn it over.

o Choose Advanced features from the Motions & gestures menu in Settings, then press Mute and touch to activate it.

Vibrations

You can manage how frequently your device vibrates.

1. From the Settings menu, choose Sounds and vibration.

2. Touch the choices to customize:

- Vibration during a call: Select from the present vibration pattern for calls.

- Notification vibration: Select from the preset vibration pattern for notification.

- System vibration: Configure the vibration amplitude and feedback for the following potential system

    - System vibration intensity: Drag the slider to modify the vibration intensity.

    - The gadget vibrates when you press and hold objects on the screen or when you push the navigation buttons.

- As you enter phone numbers, the dialing keypad vibrates.

- Samsung keyboard: This keyboard vibrates as you type on it.

- Charging: Plugging in a charger causes it to vibrate.

- While using gestures for navigation, vibrate.

- Moving the camera while zooming, changing shooting modes, and more.

• Move the sliders to adjust the strength of vibration for calls, notifications, and touch interactions.

Volume

For media, system noises, notifications, and call ringtones, adjust the volume.

o Under Settings, under Sounds and vibration > Volume, adjust the sliders for each sound type.

TIP: You may adjust the volume by using the volume keys. When pressed, a pop-up menu shows the volume level and current sound genre. After tapping the option to open it, adjust the level using the sliders for the different sound types.

Regulate media with volume key

Configure the media sound volume to be controlled by the volume keys by default rather than the type of sound that is currently playing.

1. Go to Settings and select Sounds and Vibration > Volume.

2. Tap Use Volume Keys for Media to activate this feature.

Media volume limit

Keep the device's maximum volume output at a respectable level when using Bluetooth speakers or headphones (not included).

1. From the Settings menu, choose Sounds and vibration > Volume

2. In the ⋮ More, choose Media volume limit

3. To activate this feature, tap

- Choose the highest output volume by dragging the Custom volume limit slider.

- To encrypt the volume setting, select Set volume limit PIN.

Ringtone

Make your call's ringtone stand out by selecting from the available options or entering your own. Options may vary per service provider.

1. Under the Settings menu, choose Ringtone under 🔊 Sounds and vibration.

2. Slide the slider to modify the ringtone's volume.

3. Click ➕ Add or a ringtone to select an audio file and hear a preview before using it as a ringtone.

Notification sound

Choose a standard alert sound for notifications.

1. In Settings, click Notification sound under 🔊 Sounds and vibration.

183

2. Use the slider to alter the level of the notification sound.

3. Touch an audio file to preview and select it.

TIP: The notification sounds may be customized in the App settings section to make them unique to each app.

Notifications

You may prioritize and streamline app alerts by changing which applications offer notifications and how notifications notify you

Apps notifications

Choose which applications you want to be notified about.

○ From the Settings menu, choose Notifications > App notifications to enable notifications for particular apps.

Lock screen notifications

You can choose which alerts display on the Lock screen.

○ To activate the function tap 📱 , go to Settings > 📷 Notifications > Lock screen notifications. Choose an option to modify:

• Content hidden: The alerts in the Notifications panel are not seen.

• Display content: Show notifications in the Notifications area.

• Show content when unlocked: Display notification content when the screen is unlocked.

• Notifications to show: Choose the alerts that will show up on the Lock screen

• Show on Always on display: Displaying notifications on an always-on screen is known as "showing on an always-on display."

185

Notification pop-up style

The appearance and other features of the notice can be changed.

- ○ Tap Notifications > Notification pop-up style in Settings to select a pop-up style, and then:

- • Briefly stated: Customize your notification settings.

    - App to display in-brief: Choose the apps you want to use to display brevity alerts for.

    - Edge lighting design: Choose an edge lighting design for alerts.

    - Notifications with keywords that are significant to you can be displayed in a variety of custom colors.

    - Display even while the screen is off: Whether or not to show notifications even when the device is off is up to you.

- • Detailed: Restore the Samsung Notifications settings to their original state.

Do not disturb

Do Not Disturb gives you the option to silence sounds and notifications when this mode is enabled. You can also create exceptions for people, applications, and notifications. It's also possible to set up a plan for regular tasks like sleeping or attending meetings.

○ From the Settings menu, choose Notifications > Do not disturb. After that, establish the following restrictions:

- Do not disturb: Choose this option to stop notifications and sounds.

- How long will it last?: When you manually activate Do not disturb mode, choose a default time frame.

Schedule

- Sleeping: Activate Do Not Disturb mode schedule while you are sleeping.

- Add schedule: Create a new schedule and add the days and times when your smartphone will generally be in the Do not disturb mode.

Set permission during do not disturb mode

- Calls and messages:Tap to enable exceptions to the Do not disturb setting for calls and messages.
- Application notifications: Include the applications whose alerts you want to receive in Do not disturb mode. Call, message, and chat alerts will still reach you even if you block the related apps.
- Alarms and sounds: Sounds and vibrations for alarms, events, and reminders can be enabled while Do not disturb mode is on.
- Hide notifications: By looking at your customisation choices, you can turn off notifications.

Advanced setting for notification

Services and applications can configure their notifications.

- o On the Settings menu, select 🔲 Notifications > Advanced.
- Display notifications: Modify how many alerts are displayed in the Status bar.
- Show battery percentage: The percentage of battery life left on your smartphone will be displayed in the Status bar.
- Notification history: Display notifications that you've recently received and snoozed.
- Conversation: A discussion notification can be touched and held on to prioritize, alert, or silence it.
- Floating notifications: For floating notifications to be enabled, choose the Bubbles or Smart pop-up view.
- Provide recommendations for notifications' reactions and actions: Get suggestions for relevant notifications and message actions.

189

- Display snooze button: Enable a button to be shown so you can quickly disregard notifications.

- Notification reminders: Activate and customize recurring reminders for alerts from certain apps and services. The alerts must be deleted to stop the reminders.

- App icons badges: Utilize the badges that appear on app icons to determine which apps have current alerts. By tapping, you can choose whether badges display how many unread alerts there are.

- Wireless emergency alerts: Generate tailored alert notifications using wireless emergency alerts.

Alert when phone picked up

To notify you of missed calls and texts, you can set the device to vibrate when you pick it up.

o Under the ⬡ Advanced features option under Motions and gestures in Settings, choose Alert when phone picked up to turn it on.

Display

Many display variables, like the timeout delay and font size, can all be customized.

Dark mode

You can use dark mode to darken white or bright screens and notifications to keep your eyes more comfortable at night.

- ○ Click Display in the Settings section to get the following options:

- • Light: Change the color scheme on your smartphone to one that is light (default).

- • Dark: Choose a dark color for your device's color theme.

- • Dark mode settings: The conditions under which Dark mode is employed are up to you.

- • – When required, turn on: You can program the Dark mode to run from dusk until dawn or on a custom schedule.

Display brightness

To accommodate your preferences or the available lighting, adjust the screen's brightness.

1. Choose Display from the Settings menu.

2. Make the Brightness menu more customizable:

- The Brightness slider can be moved to change the brightness level.

- Choose Adaptive brightness to have the screen brightness adjust to the surrounding light.

  - Hit Extra brightness if Adaptive brightness is disabled to increase the maximum brightness. The battery is being used more.

Tip: You may adjust the screen brightness in the Quick settings panel.

Motion smoothness

Boost the refresh rate of the screen to achieve smoother scrolling and more realistic animations.

1. Click Settings > Display > Motion Smoothness.

2. Choose an option, and then choose Apply.

Eye comfort shield

Thanks to this feature, you might sleep better and experience less eye fatigue. This function can be scheduled to automatically turn on and off.

1. In Settings, select Display > Eye Comfort Shield, and then press to activate this feature.

2. Choose an option to customize:

• Adaptive: Adaptive allows your screen's color temperature to be changed automatically based on your usage habits and the time of day.

• Custom: custom allows you to set a schedule for when the Eye Comfort Shield should be turned on.

   - Tap Set schedule and then choose from Always on, Sunset to sunrise, or Custom.

– Move the Color temperature slider to modify the filter's opacity.

- Easier control over the contrast and color tones of the display for more enjoyable viewing.

Accidental touch protection

The screen shouldn't be able to recognize touch input when the device is in a dark place, such a pocket or a bag.

- o Choose Display > Accidental touch prevention under Settings to activate the feature.

Touch sensitivity

to improve the touch sensitivity of the screen for use with screen protectors

- o Navigate to Settings and select Touch sensitivity under Display.

Show charging information

The battery level and estimated time needed to completely charge the device can be seen when the screen is off.

o Choose Show charging information under Settings > Display to enable.

Screen saver

You can show colors or images when the device is charging or when the screen is off.

1. In Settings, select Display > Screen Saver.
2. Choose one of the following options:
- None: Don't display the screen saver
- Colors: By tapping the selector, a screen with varying tones will appear.
- Photo table: Set to display a picture table to show off your photos.
- Picture frame: Use a photo frame to display your photos.

- Photos: In the "Photos" section, show pictures from your Google Photos account.

3. Choose Preview to check how the selected Screen saver works.

TIP: When a feature is highlighted, click Settings to access more options.

Raise to wake

To activate the screen, raise the device.

o Raise to wake is located under Settings > Advanced features > Motions & gestures.

Double tap to switch on screen

To activate the screen without using the Side key, double-tap it. Next select Advanced features > Motions & gestures > from the Settings menu.

Double-tap to switch off screen

Instead of using the Side key, double-tap the screen to turn it off, or select Advanced features > Motions and gestures > from the Settings menu. Double-tap the screen to turn it off before using this feature.

Keep the device screen on while viewing

Use the front camera to track your gaze so that the screen stays on while you're gazing at it.

o Choose Settings > Advanced features > Motions & gestures. Keep your screen on while you observe, then push to turn on the feature.

Using only one hand

You can change the screen layout to make operating your device with one hand possible.

1. In Settings, click One-handed mode under ⬤Advanced features.

2. After tapping ⬤ to enable the feature, choose from the list below:

- Gesture: Use the bottom edge of the screen's center to swipe downward.

- Button: Quickly press Home twice to reduce the size of the display.

Lock screen and security

You can secure your device and protect your data by setting up a screen lock.

Screen lock types

Screen lock options that offer high, medium, or no security include Swipe, Pattern, PIN, Password, and None.

NOTE: Another choice for protecting the sensitive information on your device and preventing illegal access is using biometric locks. To learn more, see biometric security.

Set a secure screen lock

To protect your smartphone, it is suggested that you utilize a secure screen lock (Pattern, PIN, or Password). For biometric locks to be configured and turned on, this is necessary.

1. From the ⬤ Lock screen > Screen lock type menu in Settings, choose a secure screen lock (Pattern, PIN, or Password).

2. Touch 〓 the lock screen to make alerts visible. The following options are available:

- Hidden content: The alerts in the Notifications panel are not seen.

- Show content: Make notifications visible in the Notifications area.

- Show content when unlocked: Display notification content when the screen is unlocked.

- Notifications to show: Choose which notifications to display on the Lock screen.

199

- Show on Always on display: Displaying notifications on an always-on screen is known as "showing on an always-on display."

3. Click Done to dismiss the menu.

4. Set up the following options for your screen lock:

- Smart lock: When reliable places or other devices are discovered, your device's smart lock automatically unlocks it. A dependable screen lock is necessary for this feature.

- Secure lock settings: Configure the preferences for your secure lock in accordance with your preferences. A dependable screen lock is necessary for this feature.

- Lock screen: Touch the lock screen to alter what is shown and how it appears.

- Widgets: Touch to change the widgets that are displayed on the Lock screen next to the clock.

- Touch and hold to edit: You can decide whether or not to allow editing of items on the

Lock screen by touching and holding the item in question.

- Always On Display: Switch on the Always On display option for the screen. For further information, see Always On Display.

- Roaming clock: A clock that moves about and shows the time both where you are and at home.

- About Lock screen: Update the software if you have a lock screen.

Find My Mobile

You may protect your device from loss or theft by allowing it to be locked, tracked online, and have your data remotely erased. Both a Samsung account and active Google location service are prerequisites for using Locate My Mobile.

Turn on Find My Mobile

Before using the Locate My Mobile feature, the options must be set and activated. To access your smartphone remotely, go to findmymobile.samsung.com.

1. Go to Settings, ⬤ Security and Privacy, Locate My Mobile, and then allow this phone to be found.

2. Tap ▶ to launch Find My Mobile to turn it on and login in to your Samsung account. The following options are available:

- Allow to find your phone: If you want this function to be able to find this phone, choose this option.

- Remote unlock: Give Samsung permission to save your PIN, pattern, or password so you may remotely unlock and control your device.

- Send last location: Enable your smartphone to communicate its most recent position to the Find My Mobile server when the battery life falls below a predetermined threshold.

Google Play Protect

It is possible to configure Google Play to regularly check your system and apps for security holes and threats.

- o Click Security and privacy > App security in Settings to access Google Play Protect.

Security update

It is easy to determine when the security software was most recently updated and whether any new improvements are accessible.

- o Navigate to Settings, tap Security and privacy > Updates > Security update, and then check to see if a newer update is available to display the most current security update that has been implemented.

Samsung pass

Use Samsung Pass to log in with your biometric data to your chosen services. You need to have your Samsung account open in order to utilize Samsung Pass.

1. Go to Settings and select Samsung Pass under ⬤Security and privacy

2. After logging in, add your biometric data to your Samsung account using Keystore for Samsung Blockchain.

   Prepare your personal blockchain key. Options may vary per service provider.

Installing unidentified apps

You have the option to approve the installation of unknown third-party apps from specific sources or apps.

1. Go to Settings > ⬤ Security and privacy > Install unrecognized apps.

2. Tap ⬤ to allow to installation from a source or an application.

NOTE: Installing unapproved third-party software could make your device and personal information more vulnerable to security attacks.

Password for factory data reset

You can request a password to reset your smartphone to its original factory settings. Options may vary per service provider.

○ Choose ⬤ Security and privacy > Further security measures > Enter a password after setting up or changing your password in the Settings section.

Activate SIM card lock

It can be protected with a PIN to prevent unauthorized use if someone tries to use your SIM card in another device. Options may vary per service provider.

- ○ Choose ⬤ Security and privacy > Further security measures > Follow the on-screen directions after configuring SIM card lock in the Settings menu.

- • Tap Lock SIM card to make the feature active.

- • By selecting Change SIM card PIN, a new PIN can be created.

Viewing password

You may briefly view the characters as you type them in password boxes.

- ○ Choose Settings > ⬤ Security and privacy > Additional security options. To activate the feature, passwords must be made available.

Device administration

Admin access to your device can be granted to security software and applications.

1. Under the Settings menu, select Security and privacy, then select Additional security settings, then select Device admin applications.

2. Tap a choice to make it available as a device administrator.

Credentials storage

The trusted security certificates on your device, which validate the reliability of servers for secure connections, can be managed.

o Under Settings, select Security and privacy > Additional security settings to get the following options:

- View security certificate: Put security certificates on the display of your device to view them.

- User certificates: See the user certificates that your device uses to identify itself in this section.

- Install from device/phone storage: With the device/storage phone's choice, install a new certificate from storage.

- Clear credentials: Change the password and purge the device's credentials of any data

- Certificate management app: To handle the information contained in your certificates, select a certificate management app.

Advanced security settings

You can use these choices to configure increased security settings for your device

- Go to Settings > Security and privacy > Additional security settings to view the options listed below.

- Agents of trust: Let connected, dependable gadgets to carry out particular tasks.

  - This option is the only one to show up when a lock screen is activated.

- Pin app: Apps can be "pinned" to the screen of your device, blocking access to other features.

- Galaxy system app update: Update the Galaxy system apps by setting up your device to download and install Samsung updates automatically.

- Security policy updates: Check for updates to keep your device secure.

Location

By combining GPS, a mobile network, and Wi-Fi, location services can pinpoint the exact location of your device.

1. From the Settings menu, select ⊙ Location.

2. To enable location services, tap ⬤

TIP: You need to activate location services for some applications for them to function.

App permissions

Give any programs access to your location data by setting up permissions.

1. Choose Location > App permissions from the Settings menu.

2. By tapping on it, choose the location permissions to give an app. There are various options available for each app.

Location services

Location services save and use the most recent location information from your device. Depending on the places you've been, certain apps might use this data to improve your search results.

1. From the Settings menu, select Location.

2. Tap an entry under Location services to see how your location data is used.

Improve accuracy

You can activate additional location-scanning tools.

1. Choose Location > Location services from the Settings menu.

2. Select connection method under Improve accuracy to remove or add from location services

- Wi-Fi scanning: Allow automatic Wi-Fi network scanning for applications and services, even when Wi-Fi is turned off

- Bluetooth scanning: Let apps to automatically find and connect to nearby Bluetooth devices, even when Bluetooth is turned off.

Recent access

A list of the programs that have requested your location is available.

1. From the Settings menu, select Location.

2. To enable location services, tap

3. Hover the mouse over a recently used item to see the app's settings.

Emergency location service

If Emergency Location Service (ELS) is available in your area and you phone or text an emergency number, your device may automatically broadcast its location to emergency response partners.

1. Choose ⬤ Emergency Location Service under Safety and Emergencies in the Settings menu.

2. Tap ⬤ this symbol to turn on the Emergency Location Service.

Accounts

You can login in and manage all of your accounts, including your email, social media, Google, and Samsung accounts.

Add an new account

You can add and sync every account you have for email, social media, and file-sharing.

1. Choose ⬤ Accounts and backup from the Settings menu, then select Manage accounts > + Add account.

2. Decide on an account type.

3. Follow the on-screen directions to enter your login details and establish the account.

- Tap Auto sync data to enable automatic account updates.

Account settings

Every account has a distinct set of settings. There may be similar parameters configured for all accounts of the same type. Account settings and functionalities are accessible for various account types in different ways.

1. Choose Manage accounts under Accounts and backup from the Settings menu.

2. Touch a profile to modify its preferences.

Delete an account

On your device, accounts can be erased.

1. Choose Manage accounts under Accounts and backup from the Settings menu.

2. After deciding on one account, choose Delete account.

Backup and restoration

Data backup to personal accounts can be configured on your device.

Samsung account

It is possible to activate data backup to your Samsung account. Options may vary per service provider.

○ Choose Accounts and backup from the Settings menu, then pick one of the options under Samsung Cloud:

- Backup of data: Configure data backup on your Samsung account.
- Restore data: Recover data by logging into your Samsung account and then restoring the data you have backed up.

Google account

You can enable Google account information backup to your Google Account.

1. On the Settings page, choose Accounts and backup.

2. Under Google Drive, select Back up data.

External storage transfer

To restore backup data, use Smart Switch, and to back up your data, use a USB storage device. To learn more, see Bring data from an old device.

o   Choose Settings > ⟳ Accounts and backup > External storage transfer.

Settings for Google

Your Google Account controls the options available when changing the Google settings on your smartphone.

o   Choose a custom option by tapping Ⓖ Google under Settings.

Date and time

The wireless network provides date and time information to your device automatically. The time and date can be manually set if there is no network coverage.

- On the Settings menu, select General management > Date and time. Alternatives include the following:

• Automatic date and time: Your wireless network will update the time and date for you. When Automatic date and time is turned off, the options below are available:

- To set the date, enter the time now.
- Set the time now by typing it in.

• Automatic time zone: Use the time zone that your cell network gives.

- Choose a time zone: Alternate your time zone.

• Change time zone in accordance with location: Get time updates according to your location.

• Use 24-hour format: Choose the 24-hour format for the time display.

Reset

Reset the device and network settings. In addition, you can reset your device to its factory defaults.

Reset all settings

Everything on your device can be reset to factory settings, with the exception of the security, language, and account settings. No changes are made to personal data.

1. Choose ⚙ General management > Reset > Reset all settings from the Settings menu in step 1.

2. When prompted, choose Reset settings and click Yes.

Reset network settings

Wi-Fi, mobile data, and Bluetooth settings can all be cleared by performing a network reset.

1. Choose ⚙ General management from the Settings menu, then select Reset > Reset network settings.

2. When prompted, choose Reset settings and click Yes.

Reset accessibility settings

The accessibility settings on a device can be reset. The accessibility options in downloaded apps and your private information are unaffected.

1. First, select Settings > General management > Reset > Reset accessibility settings.

2. When prompted, choose Reset settings and click Yes.

Reset factory data

Setting your device to factory defaults will erase all of the data on it.

Apart from system and application data and settings, Google or other account settings, and downloaded programs, this procedure completely removes ALL data on the device, including music, photos, videos, and other files.

If you sign into your device with a Google Account and set up a lock screen, Google Device Protection is automatically activated.

NOTE: It could take up to 24 hours for the new Google Account password to sync with all of the account's connected devices after you change it.

Before you reset the reset, make sure of the following:

1. Verify that the data you want to store has been transferred there.
2. Check your login information once more after logging into your Google Account.

To reset your device:

1. Choose Settings, General management, Reset, and Factory data reset.
2. To perform the reset, tap Reset and follow the prompts.
3. Set up your device by following the on-screen instructions after it resumes.

www.ingramcontent.com/pod-product-compliance
Lightning Source LLC
LaVergne TN
LVHW052059060326
832903LV00060B/2287